No-Stress Paper Piecing

by Carolyn Cullinan McCormick

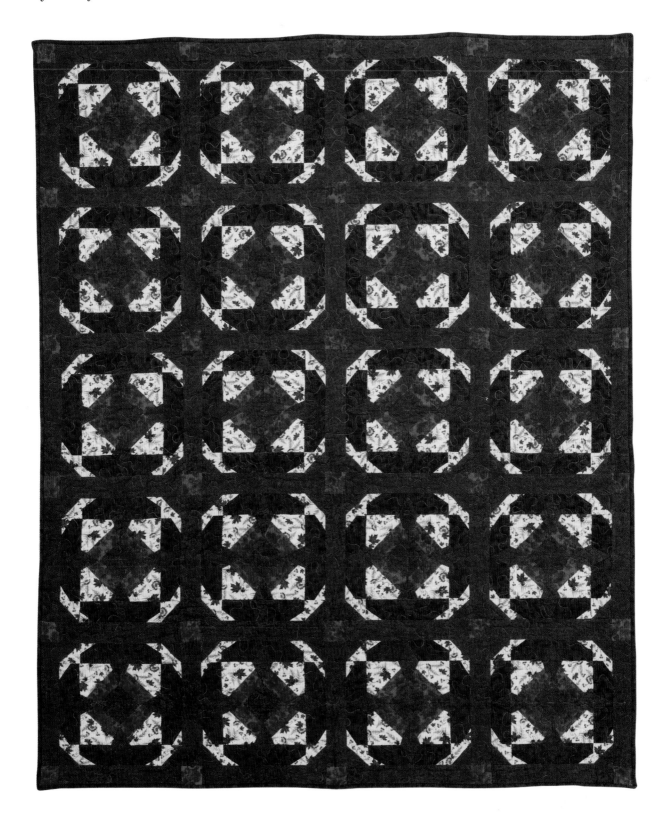

Published by

krause publications

An Imprint of F+W Publications

700 East State Street • Iola, WI 54990-0001
715-445-2214 • 888-457-2873
www.krausebooks.com

Our toll-free number to place an order or obtain a
free catalog is (800) 258-0929.

The following registered trademark terms and
companies appear in this publication:
Add-A-Quarter™, Add-Three-Eighths™

Library of Congress Catalog Number: 2006935649

ISBN 13: 978-0-89689-493-8

Designed by Rachael L. Knier
Edited by Tracy L. Conradt

Printed in China

ACKNOWLEDGMENTS

I wish to acknowledge my very grateful appreciation to
all who helped put this book together; some by testing
the quilts and others just for moral support.

Special thanks to my husband, Larry, for your never
ending love and support.

I am especially grateful for my children, Jennifer, Ryan
and Megan. I appreciate your loving support and
encouragement. Jennifer, thanks for all the help on the
computer and for making such a fun quilt. Megan, I
appreciate you testing the blocks and making them into
a wonderful sampler.

Thanks to Candy Wiza, my acquisition editor, for giving
me the opportunity to do this book and to Tracy Conradt,
my editor, for making the book so wonderful.

Thanks to book designer, Rachael Knier and photogra-
phy staff at Krause for their professional skills.

Thanks to Carol Bonetti from Castle Rock, Colo., for
making the quilt labels for all the quilts.

I want to express my heartfelt thanks to the following
family and friends for testing the quilt designs.

To my sister, Marie Huber, Glendive, Mont., thank you
for testing the blocks. I appreciate you taking the time.

Eloise's Flower Garden: Flannel quilt made by Ginny
Rafferty from Castle Rock, Colo.; quilted by Carol Willey
from Castle Rock, Colo.

Celtic Crossing: Flannel quilt made by Carol and Tom Netwal from Castle Rock, Colo.; quilted by Tracy Peterson Yadon from Manhattan, Mont.

Dresden Star: Flannel quilt made and quilted by Marilyn Vap from Castle Rock, Colo.

Jennifer's Quilt: Flannel quilt made by Claudia Harrison, Carol Herrick, Julie McClain and Mickie Morgan from Kiowa, Colo.; quilted by Pam Statley, Littleton, Colo.

Stars on Parade: Cotton quilt made by Diane Donnelly and Jennifer Lageson from Bozeman, Mont.; quilted by Tracy Peterson Yadon from Manhattan, Mont.

Wandering Trails: Cotton quilt made by Evie Scott and Nancy Orth from Kiowa, Colo., Polly Rodriquez from Bennett, Colo. and Carol Kearns from Elizabeth, Colo.; quilted by Evie Scott from Kiowa, Colo. and Polly Rodriquez from Bennett, Colo.

Winter Sky: Cotton quilt made by Maryellen Joga from Castle Rock, Colo.; quilted by Diane Varner from Elizabeth, Colo.

Lilies from the Valley: Cotton quilt made by Kathy Braun, Phyllis Holtz, Corliss Vergeldt, Maureen Simonson, Donna Braun, Dorothy Huehn, Paula Wieser from Rosholt, South Dakota; Deb Ellsworth, Millicent Hannasch, Clarice Grajczyk, JoAnn Sheldon, LaVonne Hellwig, Lorraine Stapleton, Gayle Grimsrud from Sisseton, S.D. and Ruth Bartz from Browns Valley, Minnesota; quilted by Donna Braun from Rosholt, S.D.

Cross Roads: Flannel quilt made by Polly Somers and Brenda Phillips from Sedalia, Colo. and Jeannine Glenndenning from Castle Rock Colo.; quilted by Wendy Vogel from Highlands Ranch, Colo.

Whispering Pines: Cotton quilt made by Jackie Parker from Castle Rock, Colo.; quilted by Carol Willey from Castle Rock, Colo.

Garden Path: Cotton quilt made and quilted by Julie Lilly from Monument, Colo.

Whirligig: Cotton quilt made and by Patrice Heath from Parker, Colo.

Sweet Pea: Cotton quilt made by Carol and Tom Netwal from Castle Rock, Colo., quilted by Carol Willey from Castle Rock, Colo.

Thank you, Margo Krager, the designer of the Dargate fabrics, for your donation of fabric.

Thank you Superior Thread and Auriful Thread for you donation of thread.

The long-arm quilters that quilted the quilts, Tracy Peterson Yadon, Lynnette Siegle, Jan Holden, Diane Varner, and Carol Willey, thank you.

Table of Contents

INTRODUCTION

I have to confess, I love paper piecing. My motto is "If I can't paper piece it, I won't make it." I know this is a pretty strong statement, but that's how I feel. Paper piecing allows a quilter to make designs they might not try when using other quilting techniques and with the accuracy of paper piecing, a first time quilter will get wonderful results.

The other thing I love is flannel. By combining paper piecing with flannel, you can achieve elaborate and exact designs, because the paper stabilizes the flannel and keeps it from stretching. Many quilters have not thought about using paper piecing with flannel, but I think you will love it. And there are so many wonderful flannel fabrics manufactured today. It's a terrific combination!

But then I thought, not everyone loves flannel as much as I do. And I did not want to discourage someone from making a design they found appealing.

So, I decided to provide directions in this book for both cotton and flannel. Take your choice – every quilter likes options.

This book will show you how simple it is to paper piece. If you have tried paper piecing in the past and just did not like it, you might not have been doing the technique the easiest way. The key to paper piecing is to "trim before you sew." By trimming before you sew, you remove excess fabric and leave a nice straight line. That straight line shows you exactly where to place the next piece of fabric before you sew. No more guesswork! It significantly cuts construction time and the finished blocks are especially precise.

There are thirteen designs in the book and all the designs have directions showing how to use both cotton and flannel fabric. By following the paper piecing directions I hope you will love to paper piece as much as I do. Enjoy!

DEDICATION

To my mom Eloise, I am so blessed to have you as my mother.

Love,
Carolyn

ABOUT THE AUTHOR

I was born and raised on a ranch in Eastern Montana near Glendive and currently live in Franktown, Colo., I have been married to my husband Larry for 31 years. We have two fabulous children and a wonderful daughter-in-law. Ryan, our son, works as a financial analyst in Denver. Megan, his wife works as a level 2 neo-natal nurse at Presbyterian St. Luke's Hospital. Our daughter, Jennifer, graduated from college with a degree in marketing from Hastings College and also received her nursing degree from Creighton University. The baby of the family is still our dog Jake, a 6 year old English Pointer.

Quilting has been a big part of my life for over 20 years. I worked and taught a variety of quilting and craft classes at the Patchworks in Bozeman, Mont., from 1987 to 1993. In 1993, out of frustration, I invented the Add-A-Quarter ruler.

The original idea for the Add-A-Quarter was to enable a person to automatically add a quarter inch to pieces cut with templates. Since the inception of paper-piecing, the ruler has taken on a whole new role in the quilting world and is a standard tool for making paper-pieced items. I have been distributing the Add-A-Quarter since 1995.

Quilting has taken me down many roads and given me many opportunities. I have met many wonderful and gifted people! The talent I see in the quilting community continues to amaze me.

— Carolyn

Above are the 12" Add-A-Quarter and 12" Add-Three-Eighths rulers which Carolyn invented and now manufactures.

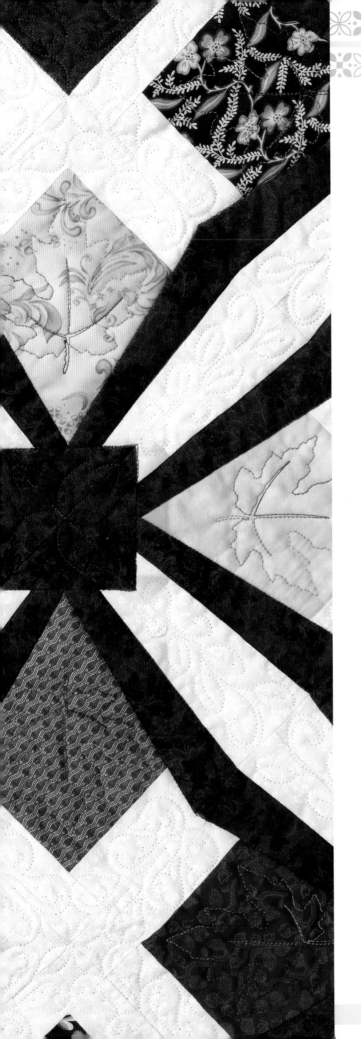

How to Paper Piece

WHY PAPER PIECE?

Paper piecing is great for beginners as well as experienced quilters. One can make a wonderful quilt on their very first try since complicated patterns are broken down into easily managed steps. Sewing the fabric to paper makes matching points relatively easy and the paper stabilizes the fabric; that is especially important when using flannel.

BEFORE YOU START TO SEW:

Make copies of the patterns that you are going to use from the CD. If you do not have a computer contact a friend, relative or a photo copy shop to print the originals off the CD. Use the set of originals for copying on the photo copier. Make all of your copies from the same original and use the same copy machine. All copy machines distort to some extent so check your patterns by holding the original and the copy together with a light source behind the two sheets of paper. Make as many copies as necessary. It's nice to have a few extras in case you make an error. Use the lightest weight paper you can find. The heavier the paper the more difficult it is to remove.

After making all your copies, trim each pattern leaving ⅛" to ¼" on all sides. Do not trim on the line.

Set the stitch length on your sewing machine to 18-20 stitches per inch. On some machines that will be a 1½. The smaller stitches make it easier to rip off the paper.

Place a piece of muslin or scrap fabric on your ironing board. When you press the pieces, the ink from the copies may transfer onto your ironing board cover.

It is helpful to have something white to place your pattern face down on. It could be a white sewing table or just a piece of white paper. Placing your pattern on something white allows the lines to show through, making it easier to place your first fabric.

YOU ARE NOW READY TO START:

Here is a familiar pattern.

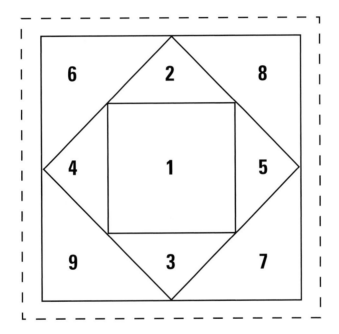

Instead of templates with seam allowances as many of us are used to seeing, we have lines and numbers. The lines indicate where to sew and the numbers indicate the sequence in which to sew. The only seam allowances that are shown are the ones that go around a block or a unit.

The lines and numbers are printed on the front of the pattern. This is the side to sew on.

The back of the pattern is the blank side. This is where the fabric will be placed.

Follow the directions on the cutting chart for strip cutting using the full width of the fabric. Then cut the strips into the size needed. Mark each stack of fabric after it is cut (example: 2" x 4"). This will make it easier when it comes time to sew your fabric onto your pattern; you will not have to re-think what fabric goes where. Always make sure the piece of fabric you are using is at least ¼" larger for cotton and ⅜" larger for flannel all the way around the foundation pattern.

Place fabric number 1 right side up on the blank side of the pattern. You may either pin the piece in place or use double-sided tape to hold the fabric in place. The tape makes the fabric lie flat on the paper. The pin can make a small rise in the paper.

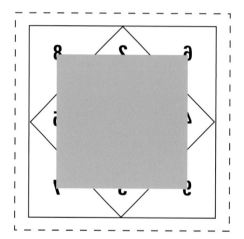

Turn the foundation pattern over, look through the paper towards your light source or place pattern on white and make sure the fabric extends over the lines on each side by at least ¼" for cotton and ⅜" for flannel.

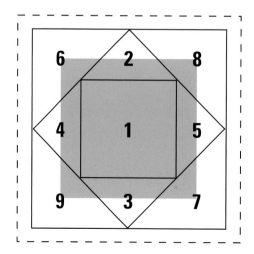

Place your template plastic or an index card on the sewing line between piece number 1 and piece number 2. Fold back the foundation pattern over the edge of the template plastic. You will see the excess fabric from piece number 1.

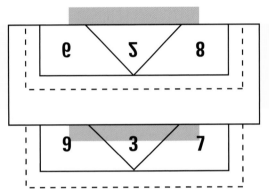

Place the Add-A-Quarter ruler for cotton or if you are using flannel use the Add-Three-Eighths ruler up against the fold of the foundation paper with the lip side down. If you do not have an Add-A-Quarter or an Add-Three-Eighths you may use a regular ruler. Be very careful because a regular ruler may slip cutting into your pattern. Use the rotary cutter to trim the extra fabric from piece number 1. You will now have a straight line to help you place fabric piece number 2.

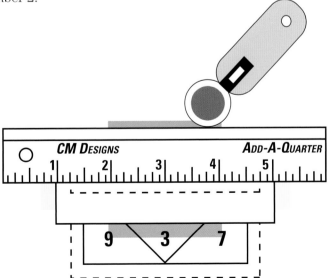

Next, place position number 2 fabric of the pattern on the trimmed edge of piece number 1 with the right sides facing each other.

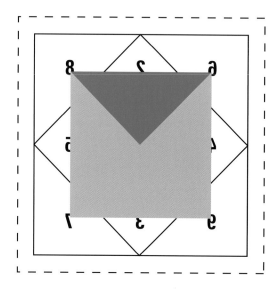

Turn the foundation paper over and stitch on the line between piece number 1 and piece number 2. Sew a few stitches before the line begins and a few stitches after the line ends. Make sure piece number 2 does not slip.

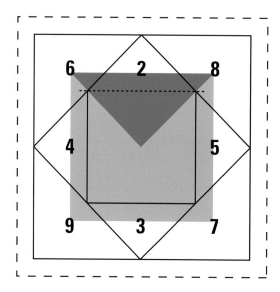

Flip the paper over and open piece number 2. Press using a dry iron.

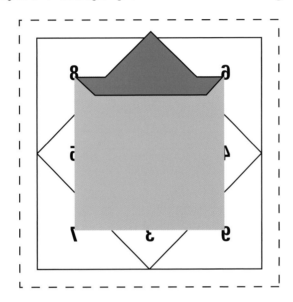

Fold the foundation paper back along the line between piece number 1 and piece number 3 using the template plastic or the index card. Butt the ruler of your choice up against the paper and trim the excess fabric.

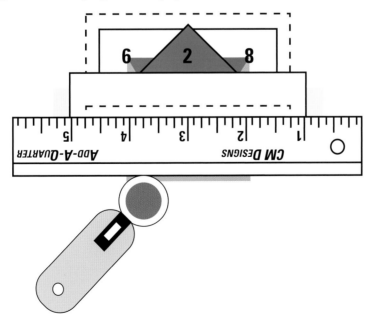

Turn the foundation over and position fabric piece number 3, being careful not to displace your fabric. Sew on the line between number 1 and number 3.

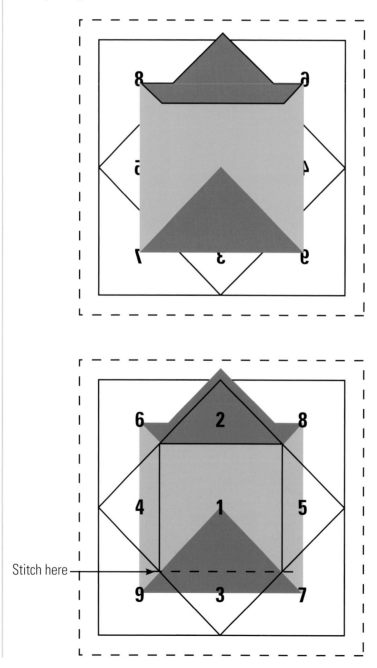

Continue sewing each piece in place in the numeric order given until all the pieces are sewn in place and each unit is complete.

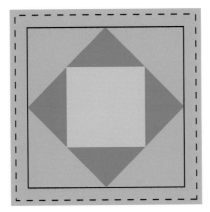

After all the pieces are sewn onto the foundation, you will be ready to trim the edges. Line up the ruler with the solid line on the foundation. You will need a ¼" seam allowance for cotton and a ⅜" seam allowance for flannel around the entire block. <u>Never trim on the solid line!</u> Trim off the excess fabric using your rotary cutter.

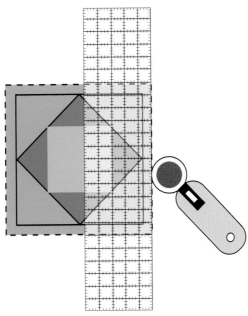

If you are paper piecing a block that is made up of multiple units, the time has come to sew them together. If you have points that need to match, carefully push a positioning pin straight through the top layer of your pattern, then match the bottom layer and push straight through. Leaving the positioning pin in place, pin on both sides.

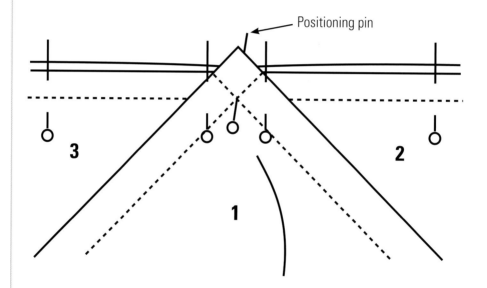

Do not twist the positioning pin to pin; this will distort your points. Pin the rest of the seam like normal. Pull pins out of the seam line just before the needle reaches them, this will also help decrease distortion.

When the block is finished, do not remove the paper! It is best to join the blocks before you remove the paper. This gives you a line to follow when you sew the blocks together and the paper helps keep the integrity of the block because when paper piecing, you are not placing your fabric on the straight of grain. Remove the paper after the blocks are sewn together. You might want to remove the really small pieces with a pair of tweezers.

A FEW SUGGESTIONS:

If you must remove your stitches and the paper foundation separates on the sewing line, use a piece of clear tape to repair the pattern.

Sometimes you will notice the stitches from the previously sewn fabric when you fold back the foundation. If this happens, just pull the foundation away from the fabric and trim using the ruler.

After you have sewn two units together and pressed, remove the paper from the back side of the seam allowance. This will reduce some of the bulk.

To help speed up your paper piecing, place all of your position 1 pieces on multiple units at the same time. Trim and sew multiple units at the same time. Some pieces you may even chain piece.

By placing your pattern face down on a white piece of paper, you will be able to see the outline of the design for placement of your first piece.

PRESSING SUGGESTIONS:

Pressing is an important part of paper piecing and done correctly will help to insure a more satisfactory quilt. Here are some suggestions to follow:

Use a hot dry iron. Steam will make the paper curl.

Place a piece of muslin on your ironing board to protect it from ink that may come off when pressing.

Always press with the paper side down on your ironing board. If you press on the paper side ink will be transferred to the iron and then onto your fabric leaving black smudges.

The traditional way to press is always to the dark side. With paper piecing you will not be able to always follow this rule. I always press the seams to one side. Pressing this way adds strength to your quilt and helps to distribute the bulk. This is very important especially when working with flannel. Keep this rule in mind when you are sewing units together. By creating this opposing seam it will be easier to match your points or corners and distribute the bulk of the fabric at the same time.

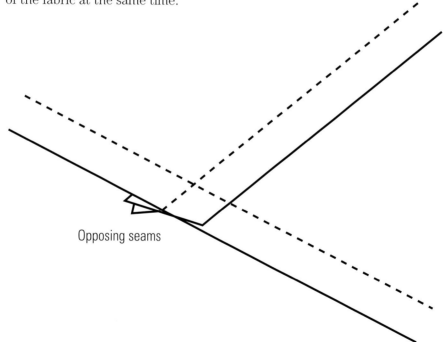

Opposing seams

ASSEMBLING YOUR QUILT

SETTING TRIANGLES AND CORNER TRIANGLES

If your quilt requires setting triangles and corner triangles follow the directions for each quilt for the correct size to cut listed under cutting directions.

For setting triangles cut the square from corner to corner two times to give you quarter-square triangles.

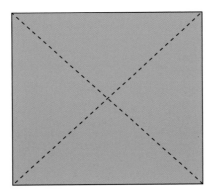

When making corner triangles cut the square on the diagonal one time from corner to corner for half-square triangles.

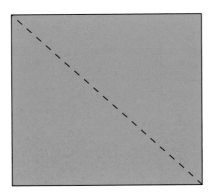

SASHING AND CORNERSTONES:

Follow the directions in the cutting section.

How to measure and sew borders:

All the borders in this book are strips with straight cut seams. Cut the width of your fabric and follow the cutting chart for cutting requirements.

Measure your quilt from side to side in the center of the quilt. If your measurement is larger then 40" for cotton and 38" for flannel you will have to piece the border. Piece the border strips together by sewing a straight seam. Press. Cut two of the border strips to match the measurement. Pin the border on by pinning one end and then the other end. Start in the middle and pin in both directions. This will give you the opportunity to ease where necessary to keep your quilt square. If the paper is still on the fabric when sewing on the first pinned border, sew with paper facing up. This will give you a stitching line to follow and also will keep your border from stretching. Press.

Measure your quilt from top to bottom in the center of the quilt. Piece two strips together by sewing a straight seam. Press. Cut two of the border strips to match the measurement. Pin and sew into place as above. Press.

If there is more than one border follow the same procedure as above. Sew on the top and bottom first and then adding the sides. When adding borders; try using your walking foot to help keep the fabric from stretching.

QUILTING:

You may quilt your quilt yourself or do like I do and hire a professional long-arm quilter. I like to have a professional quilt my quilts for two reasons. One, I don't have to do it; therefore, I can move on to my next project. Two, most are very good at what they do and have a better idea of what thread and design will enhance your quilt.

BINDING:

Follow the cutting directions to cut the number of strips required for your quilt. Trim the ends at a 45-degree angle. Sew the strips together on the diagonal using a ¼" seam allowance for cotton and ⅜" for flannel.

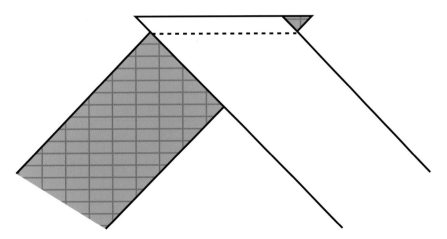

Press the seams.

Fold the strips in half lengthwise, wrong sides together and press. Turn one end of the strip under ¼" for cotton and ⅜" for flannel and press.

Starting with the end that has been turned under, line up the raw edges of the binding with the quilt top edge. Start to sew a few inches down from the end using ¼" seam allwance for cotton and ⅜" for flannel. A walking foot works great when putting on binding. To miter your corners, stop sewing ¼" from the edge of the quilt for cotton and ⅜" from the edge of the quilt for flannel.

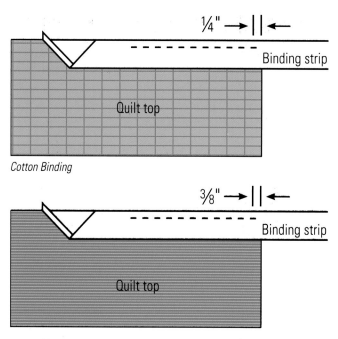

Cotton Binding

Flannel Binding

Turn quilt and back stitch off the edge. Fold the binding back on itself, even with the quilt top edge, making a 45-degree angle.

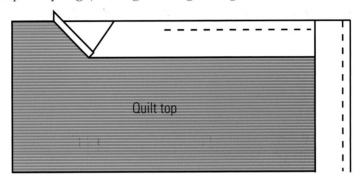

Continue sewing with the appropriate seam allowance. Repeat the sewing and mitering all the way around the quilt. When you reach the beginning of the binding, overlap the binding by about 1". Cut the excess off at a 45 degree angle. Insert the end of the binding into the fold and continue sewing.

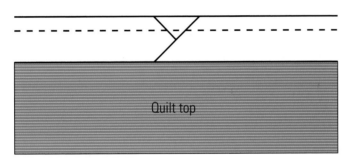

Fold the binding to the back of the quilt, mitering the corners and pin. Stitch binding on by hand.

Eloise's Flower Garden

Cotton quilt made by Carolyn Cullinan McCormick; quilted by Carol Willey, Castle Rock, Colo.

Quilt Size: 59" x 76½" quilted
18 – 12" Blocks
Number of Copies Needed:
Unit A – 72

Refer to How to Paper Piece on page 9 for any
instructions on cutting, assembling, quilting and binding.

Position Chart

FABRIC	POSITION	COTTON	FLANNEL
Unit A – Make 72			
Printed	1	5" x 5"	5¼" x 5¼"
Background	2	1¾" x 3¾"	2" x 4"
Background	3	1¾" x 4¾"	2" x 5"
Green	4, 5	2" x 6¼"	2¼" x 6½"
Background	6, 7	1¾" x 5½"	2" x 5¾"
Green	8	3½" x 3½" ◩	3¾" x 3¾" ◩

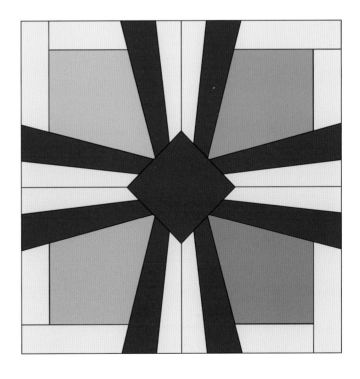

Cotton Fabric Requirements

Background:	
Blocks	2¼ yd.
Green:	
Blocks	2 yd.
Setting & Corner Triangles	1½ yd.
2nd Border	1 yd.
Total	4½ yd.
Various Prints:	72 – 5" squares
Gold:	
1st Border	⅜ yd.
Maroon:	
Binding	⅝ yd.
Backing:	4 yd. – Crosswise
	5 yd. – Lengthwise
Batting:	2 yd. 90" wide

Cotton Cutting Directions

Note: Strips are cut the width of the fabric; 40" for cotton.

From the background fabric, cut:

Unit A-2

- 4 – 3¾" strips. Cut the strips into 72 – 1¾" x 3¾" rectangles.

Unit A-3

- 4 – 4¾" strips. Cut the strips into 72 – 1¾" x 4¾" rectangles.

Units A-6 and 7

- 7 – 5½" strips. Cut the strips into 144 – 1¾" x 5½" rectangles.

From the green fabric, cut:

Unit A-8

- 4 – 3½" strips. Cut the strips into 36 – 3½" squares. Cut the squares into half-square triangles.

Units A-4 and 5

- 8 – 6¼" strips. Cut the strips into 144 – 2" x 6¼" rectangles.

From various printed fabric, cut:

Unit A-1

- 72 – 5" squares.

Triangles, Borders and Binding:

From the green fabric, cut:

Setting Triangles

- 2 – 18¼" strips. Cut the strips into 3 – 18¼" squares. Cut the squares on the diagonal twice.

Corner Triangles

- 1 – 9⅜" strip. Cut the strip into 2 – 9⅜" squares. Cut the squares into half-square triangles.

2nd Border

- 7 – 4" strips.

From the gold fabric, cut:

1st Border

- 7 – 1½" strips.

From the maroon fabric, cut:

Binding

- 7 – 2½" strips.

Flannel Cutting Directions

Note: Strips are cut the width of the fabric; 38" for flannel.

From the background fabric, cut:

Unit A-2
- 4 – 4" strips. Cut the strips into 72 – 2" x 4" rectangles.

Unit A-3
- 4 – 5" strips. Cut the strips into 72 – 2" x 5" rectangles.

Units A-6 and 7
- 8 – 5¾" strips. Cut the strips into 144 – 2" x 5¾" rectangles.

From the green fabric, cut:

Unit A-8
- 4 – 3¾" strips. Cut the strips into 36 – 3¾" squares. Cut the squares into half-square triangles.

Units A-4 and 5
- 9 – 6½" strips. Cut the strips into 144 – 2¼" x 6½" rectangles.

From various printed fabric, cut:

Unit A-1
- 72 – 5¼" squares.

Triangles, Borders and Binding:

From the green fabric, cut:
Setting Triangles
- 2 – 18⅞" strips. Cut the strips into 3 – 18⅞" squares. Cut the squares on the diagonal twice.

Corner Triangles
- 1 – 9¾" strip. Cut the strip into 2 – 9¾" squares. Cut the squares into half-square triangles.

2nd Border
- 7 – 4¼" strips.

From the gold fabric, cut:
1st Border
- 7 – 1¾" strips.

From the maroon fabric, cut:
Binding
- 7 – 2¾" strips.

Flannel Fabric Requirements

Background:	
Blocks	2⅝ yd.
Green:	
Blocks	2⅜ yd.
Setting & Corner Triangles	1⅝ yd.
2nd Border	1 yd.
	Total 5 yd.
Various Prints:	72 – 5¼" squares
Gold:	
1st Border	½ yd.
Maroon:	
Binding	¾ yd.
Backing:	4 yd. – Crosswise
	5 yd. – Lengthwise
Batting:	2 yd. 90" wide

Sewing Directions

1. Following the position chart sew, all fabric onto the units A.
2. Trim the units leaving a ¼" seam allowance for cotton and ⅜" for flannel.
3. Sew units together following the diagram on how to assemble the block.

4. After sewing units A together press all seams in the same direction. When sewing four units together opposite seams will form, reducing the bulk.

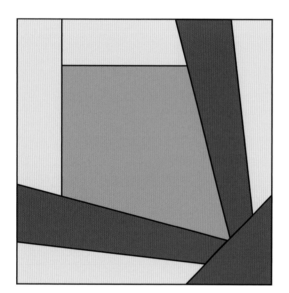

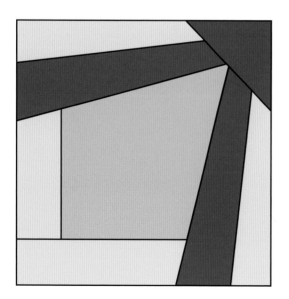

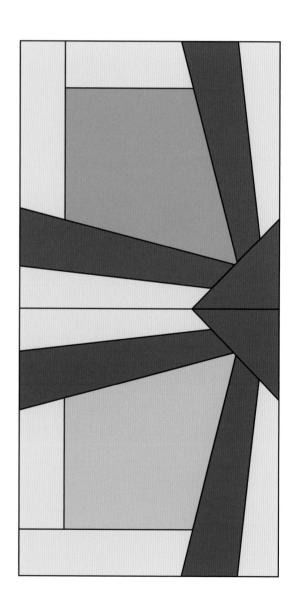

5. Remove only the paper on the back side of the seam allowance; leave the remaining paper on until the block has been sewn to another block or sashings have been added.

6. Sew all units together making 18 blocks.

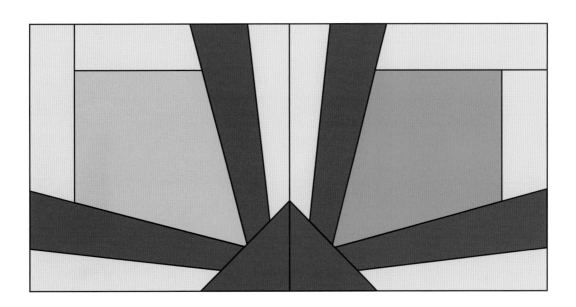

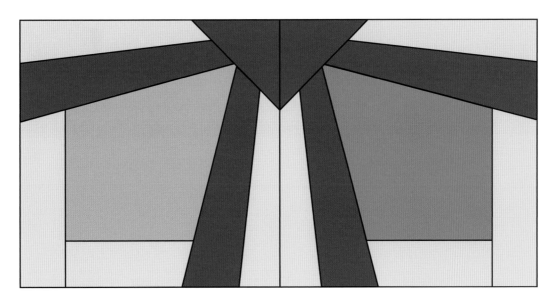

Assembling the Quilt

1. Referring to the diagram, sew the rows of blocks, setting triangles and corner triangles on point using a ¼" seam allowance for cotton and ⅜" for flannel. Remember to follow the pressing arrows; this will help when sewing the rows together.

2. Remove the paper from the center of the quilt but do not remove the paper from the outside edges until the borders have been sewn on.

3. Add the first border to the top and bottom using a ¼" seam allowance for cotton and ⅜" for flannel. Press towards the border. Add the sides; press towards the border.

4. Sew on the second border following the same sequence.

5. Remove the remaining paper.

6. Quilt as desired.

7. Trim off excess batting and backing.

8. Sew on binding.

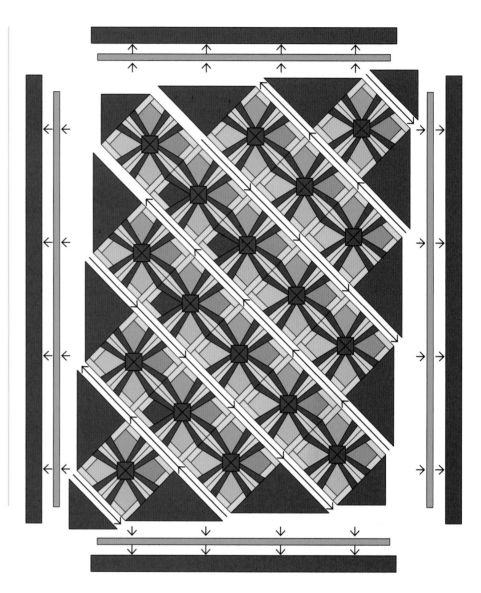

Flannel quilt made by Ginny Rafferty, Castle Rock, Colo. and machine quilted by Carol Willey, Castle Rock, Colo.

Celtic Crossing

Cotton quilt made by Carolyn Cullinan McCormick; quilted by Carol Willey, Castle Rock, Colo.

Quilt Size: 57" x 71" quilted
20 – 12" Blocks
Number of Copies Needed:
***Unit A – 80*
***Note: Use legal size paper (8½" x 14")*

Refer to How to Paper Piecing on page 9 for any instructions on cutting, assembling, quilting and binding.

Position Chart

FABRIC	POSITION	COTTON	FLANNEL
Unit A – Make 80			
Green	1	5" x 5"	5¼" x 5¼"
Red	2, 3	2" x 5¾"	2¼" x 6"
Background	4, 5	3½" x 5"	3¾" x 5¼"
Red	6, 7	1½" x 4"	1¾" x 4¼"
Green	8, 9	3¼" x 3¼" ◩	3½" x 3½" ◩
Red	10	3½" x 3½" ◩	3¾" x 3¾" ◩

Cotton Fabric Requirements

Background:		
Blocks	2⅜ yd.	
Binding	⅝ yd.	
	Total 3 yd.	
Red:		
Blocks	2¾ yd.	
Sashing	1⅜ yd.	
	Total 4⅛ yd.	
Green:		
Blocks	2¼ yd.	
Cornerstones	¼ yd.	
	Total 2½ yd.	
Backing:	4 yd. – Crosswise	
	4½ yd. – Lengthwise	
Batting:	2 yd. 90" wide	

Cotton Cutting Directions

Note: *Strips are cut the width of the fabric; 40" for cotton.*

From the background fabric, cut:
Units A-4 and 5
- 15 – 5" strips. Cut the strips into 160 – 3½" x 5" rectangles.

From the red fabric, cut:
Unit A-10
- 4 – 3½" strips. Cut the strips into 40 – 3½" squares. Cut the squares into half-square triangles.

Units A-6 and 7
- 7 – 4" strips. Cut the strips into 160 – 1½" x 4" rectangles.

Units A-2 and 3
- 8 – 5¾" strips. Cut the strips into 160 – 2" x 5¾" rectangles.

From the green fabric, cut:
Units A-8 and 9
- 7 – 3¼" strips. Cut the strips into 80 – 3¼" squares. Cut the squares into half-square triangles.

Unit A-1
- 10 – 5" strips. Cut the strips into 80 – 5" squares.

Sashing, Cornerstones and Binding:

From the red fabric, cut:
Sashing
- 17 – 2½" strips. Cut the strips into 49 – 2½" x 12½" rectangles.

From the green fabric, cut:
Corner Stones
- 2 – 2½" strips. Cut the strips into 30 – 2½" squares.

From the background fabric, cut:
Binding
- 7 – 2½" strips.

Flannel Cutting Directions

Note: Strips are cut the width of the fabric; 38" for flannel.

From the background fabric, cut:

Units A-4 and 5

- 16 – 5¼" strips. Cut the strips into 160 – 3¾" x 5¼" rectangles.

From the red fabric, cut:

Unit A-10

- 4 – 3¾" strips. Cut the strips into 40 – 3¾" squares. Cut the squares into half-square triangles.

Units A-6 and 7

- 8 – 4¼" strips. Cut the strips into 160 – 1¾" x 4¼" rectangles.

Units A-2 and 3

- 10 – 6" strips. Cut the strips into 160 – 2¼" x 6" rectangles.

From the green fabric, cut:

Units A-8 and 9

- 8 – 3½" strips. Cut the strips into 80 – 3½" squares. Cut the squares into half-square triangles.

Unit A-1

- 12 – 5¼" strips. Cut the strips into 80 – 5¼" squares.

Sashing, Cornerstones and Binding:

From the red fabric, cut:

Sashing

17 – 2¾" strips. Cut the strips into 49 – 2¾" x 12¾" rectangles.

From the green fabric, cut:

Corner Stones

3 – 2¾" strips. Cut the strips into 30 – 2¾" squares.

From the background fabric, cut:

Binding

7 – 2¾" strips.

Flannel Fabric Requirements

Background:	
Blocks	2⅝ yd.
Binding	¾ yd.
	Total 3⅜ yd.
Red:	
Blocks	3¼ yd.
Sashing	1½ yd.
	Total 4¾ yd.
Green:	
Blocks	2¾ yd.
Cornerstones	⅜ yd.
	Total 3⅛ yd.
Backing:	4 yd. – Crosswise
	4½ yd. – Lengthwise
Batting:	2 yd. 90" wide

Sewing Directions

1. Following the position chart sew all fabric onto the units A.

2. Trim the units leaving a ¼" seam allowance for cotton and ⅜" for flannel.

3. Sew units together following the diagram on how to assemble the block.

4. After sewing units A together press all seams in the same direction. Sewing four units together opposite seams will form, reducing the bulk.

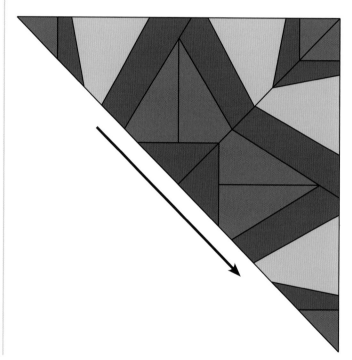

5. Remove only the paper on the back side of the seam allowance; leave the remaining paper on until you sew the block to another block or have added sashing.

6. Sew all units together making 20 blocks.

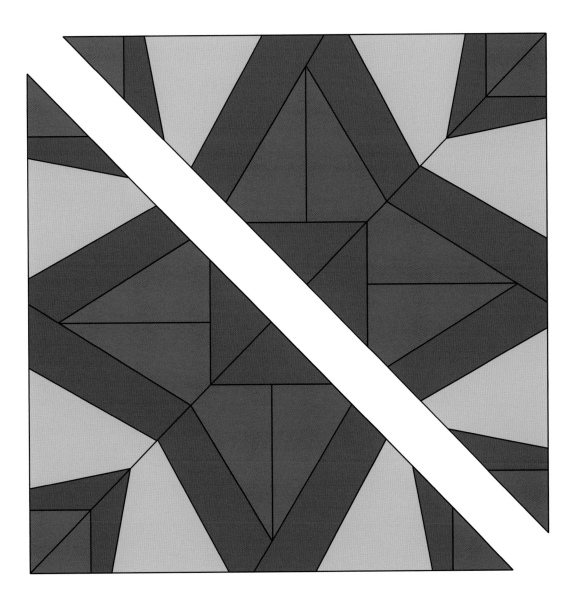

Assembling the Quilt

1. Referring to the diagram, sew sashing between the rows of blocks using a ¼" seam allowance for cotton and ⅜" for flannel.

2. Follow pressing arrows, pressing towards the sashing.

3. Sew cornerstones and sashing together using a ¼" seam allowance for cotton and ⅜" for flannel.

4. Press towards the sashing. Follow pressing arrows.

5. Assemble quilt following diagram using a ¼" seam allowance for cotton and ⅜" for flannel.

6. Remove the paper.

7. Quilt as desired.

8. Trim off excess batting and backing.

9. Sew on binding.

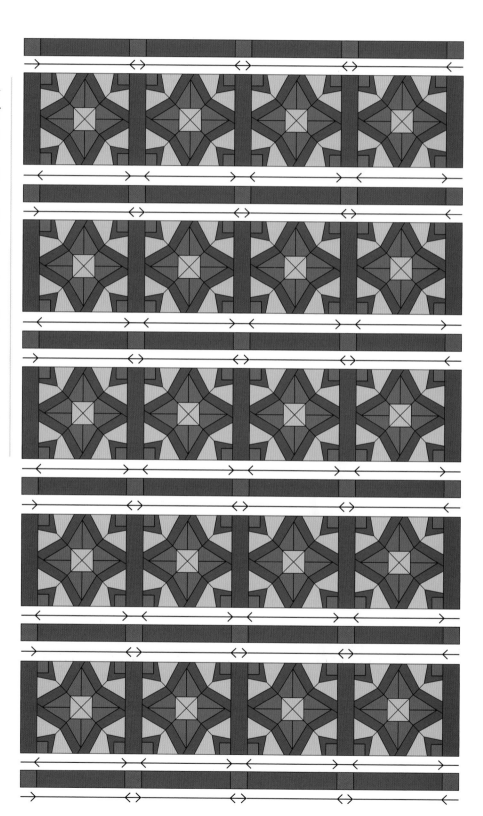

Flannel quilt by Carol and Tom Netwal, Castle Rock, Colo. and machine quilted by Tracy Peterson Yadon, Manhattan, Mont.

Dresden Star

Cotton quilt made by Carolyn Cullinan McCormick; quilted by Lynnette Siegle and Jan Holden, Glendive, Mont.

Quilt Size: 65½" x 85" quilted
12 – 12" Blocks
Number of Copies Needed:
Unit A – 48
Unit B – 48

Refer to How to Paper Piecing on page 9 for any
instructions on cutting, assembling, quilting and binding.

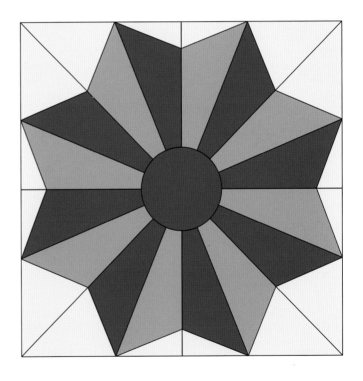

Position Chart

FABRIC	POSITION	COTTON	FLANNEL
Unit A – Make 48			
Dark Blue	1	3" x 6¼"	3¼" x 6½"
Medium Blue	2	3" x 6¼"	3¼" x 6½"
Background	3	3½" x 4¼"	3¾" x 4½"
Background	4	2" x 4"	2¼" x 4¼"
Unit B – Make 48			
Dark Blue	1	3" x 6¼"	3¼" x 6½"
Medium Blue	2	3" x 6¼"	3¼" x 6½"
Background	3	3½" x 4¼"	3¾" x 4½"
Background	4	2" x 4"	2¼" x 4¼"

Cotton Fabric Requirements

Background:	
Blocks	2⅛ yd.
Blank Blocks and Triangles	2¼ yd.
Total	**4⅜ yd.**
Dark Blue:	
Blocks	2 yd.
Cornerstones	⅜ yd.
2nd Border	1¼ yd.
Total	**3⅝ yd.**
Medium Blue:	
Blocks	1⅝ yd.
Sashing	1⅜ yd.
1st Border	¾ yd.
Binding	¾ yd.
Total	**4½ yd.**
Backing:	5¼ yd. – Lengthwise
Batting:	2 yd. 90" wide

Cotton Cutting Directions

Note: Strips are cut the width of the fabric; 40" for cotton.

From background fabric, cut:
Units A-4 and B-4
- 6 – 4" strips. Cut the strips into 96 – 2" x 4" rectangles.

Units A-3 and B-3
- 10 – 4¼" strips. Cut the strips into 96 – 3½" x 4¼" rectangles.

From the dark blue fabric, cut:
Units A-1 and B-1
- 8 – 6¼" strips. Cut the strips into 96 – 3" x 6¼" rectangles.

From the medium blue fabric, cut:
Units A-2 and B-2
- 8 – 6¼" strips. Cut the strips into 96 – 3" x 6¼" rectangles.

Center Circle:

From the dark blue fabric, cut:
- 3 – 3¾" strips. Cut the strips into 24 – 3¾" squares. Use for the center front and back circle.

Sashing and Cornerstones:

From the medium blue fabric, cut:
Sashing
- 16 – 2½" strips. Cut the strips into 48 – 2½" x 12½" rectangles.

From the dark blue fabric, cut:
Corner Stones
- 2 – 2½" strips. Cut the strips into 17 – 2½" squares.

- 1 – 4" strip. Cut the strips into 4 – 4" squares. Cut from corner to corner twice to get quarter square triangles. You will need 14.

Blank Blocks, Triangles, Borders and Binding:

From the background fabric, cut:
Blank Blocks
- 2 – 12½" strips. Cut the strips into 6 – 12½" squares.

Setting triangles
- 2 – 18¼" strips. Cut the strips into 3 – 18¼" squares. Cut the squares on the diagonal twice.

Corner Triangles
- 1 – 9⅜" strip. Cut the strip into 2 – 9⅜" squares. Cut the squares into half-square triangles.

From the medium blue fabric, cut:
1st Border
- 8 – 2½" strips.

Binding
- 8 – 2½" strips

From the dark blue fabric, cut:
2nd Border
- 8 – 4½" strips

Flannel Cutting Directions

Note: Strips are cut the width of the fabric; 38" for flannel.

From background fabric, cut:
Units A-4 and B-4
- 6 – 4¼" strips. Cut the strips into 96 – 2¼" x 4¼" rectangles.

Units A-3 and B-3
- 10 – 4½" strips. Cut the strips into 96 – 3¾" x 4½" rectangles.

From the dark blue fabric, cut:
Units A-1 and B-1
- 9 – 6½" strips. Cut the strips into 96 – 3¼" x 6½" rectangles.

From the medium blue fabric, cut:
Units A-2 and B-2
- 9 – 6½" strips. Cut the strips into 96 – 3¼" x 6½" rectangles.

Center Circle:

From the dark blue fabric, cut:
- 3 – 4" strips. Cut the strips into 24 – 4" squares. Use for the center front and back circle.

Sashing and Cornerstones:

From the medium blue fabric, cut:
Sashing
- 16 – 2¾" strips. Cut the strips into 48 – 2¾" x 12¾" rectangles.

From the dark blue fabric, cut:
Corner Stones
- 2 – 2¾" strips. Cut the strips into 17 – 2¾" squares.

- 1 – 4½" strip. Cut the strip into 4 – 4½" squares. Cut from corner to corner twice to get quarter square triangles. You will need 14.

Blank Blocks, Triangles, Borders and Binding:

From the background fabric, cut:
Blank Blocks
- 2 – 12¾" strips. Cut the strips into 6 – 12¾" squares.

Setting triangles
- 2 – 18⅞" strips. Cut the strips into 3 – 18⅞" squares. Cut the squares on the diagonal twice.

Corner Triangles
- 1 – 9¾" strip. Cut the strip into 2 – 9¾" squares. Cut the squares into half-square triangles.

From the medium blue fabric, cut:
1st Border
- 8 – 2¾" strips.

Binding
- 8 – 2¾" strips

From the dark blue fabric, cut:
2nd Border
8 – 4¾" strips

Flannel Fabric Requirements

Background:	
Blocks	2¼ yd.
Blank Blocks and Triangles	2¼ yd.
	Total 4½ yd.
Dark Blue:	
Blocks	2¼ yd.
Cornerstones	⅜ yd.
2nd Border	1¼ yd.
	Total 3⅞ yd.
Medium Blue:	
Blocks	1⅞ yd.
Sashing	1½ yd.
1st Border	¾ yd.
Binding	¾ yd.
	Total 4⅞ yd.
Backing:	5¼ yd. – Lengthwise
Batting:	2 yd. 90" wide

Sewing Directions

1. Following the position chart, sew all fabric onto units A and units B.

2. Trim the units leaving a ¼" seam allowance for cotton and ⅜" for flannel.

3. Sew units A and units B together.

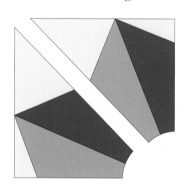

4. Press all the same direction.

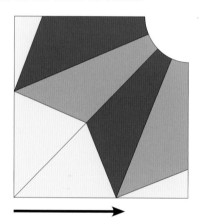

5. Sew two units AB together.

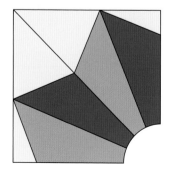 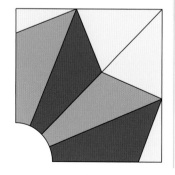

6. Press all the same direction.

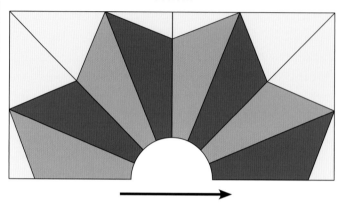

7. Sew all the units together making 12 blocks.

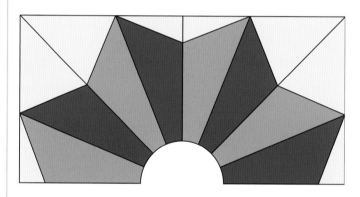

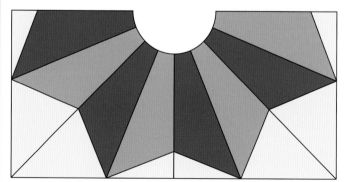

8. Remove only the paper on the back side of the seam allowance and a small amount from the center of the block. Leave the remaining paper on until the blocks have been sewn to the sashing.

9. Using the 3¾" dark blue squares for cotton or the 4" dark blue squares for flannel place two squares right sides together.

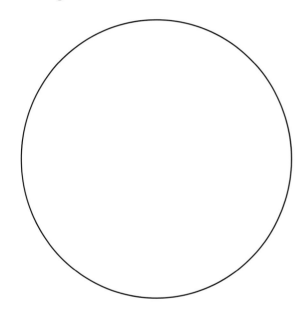

10. Make a template out of the circle that is provided.

11. Place the template on the back side of the fabric and trace around the template using a pencil or a marking pen. You will need to do this 12 times, one set for each block.

12. Sew on the traced line.

13. Trim to ¼" for cotton and ⅜" for flannel.

14. Cut an X, just on one side. Turn right sides out. Press.

15. Center and sew onto the blocks by using the stitch of your choice.

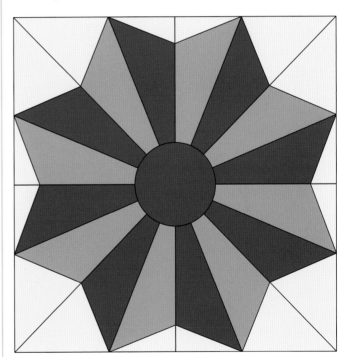

Assembling the Quilt

1. Referring to the diagram, set blocks, setting triangles and corner triangles on point. Sew sashing between the rows of blocks using a ¼" seam allowance for cotton and ⅜" for flannel.

2. Press towards the sashing. Follow pressing arrows.

3. Sew cornerstones and sashing together using a ¼" seam allowance for cotton and ⅜" for flannel.

4. Press towards the sashing. Follow pressing arrows.

5. Sew rows together using a ¼" seam allowance for cotton and ⅜" for flannel.

6. Remove the paper from the quilt.

7. Add the first border to the top and bottom using a ¼" seam allowance for cotton and ⅜" for flannel; press towards the border. Add the sides; press towards the border.

8. Sew on the second border following the same sequence.

9. Quilt as desired.

10. Trim off excess batting and backing.

11. Sew on binding.

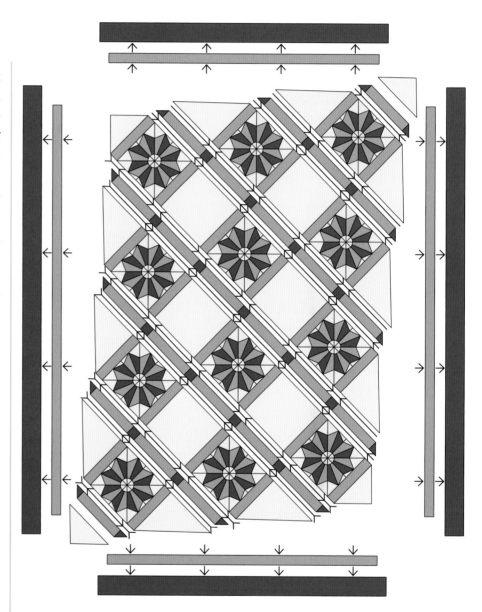

Flannel quilt pieced and machine quilted by Marilyn Vap, Castle Rock, Colo.

Jennifer's Quilt

Cotton quilt made by Carolyn Cullinan McCormick; quilted by Carol Willey, Castle Rock, Colo.

Quilt Size: 57" x 70½" quilted
20 – 12" Blocks
Number of Copies Needed:
Unit A – 80
Unit B – 40
***Unit C – 40**
***Note: Use legal size paper (8½" x 14")*

Refer to How to Paper Piecing on page 9 for any
instructions on cutting, assembling, quilting and binding.

Position Chart

FABRIC	POSITION	COTTON	FLANNEL
Unit A – Make 80			
Floral	1	5½" x 5½" ◸	5¾" x 5¾" ◸
Rose	2	2¼" x 4½"	2½" x 4¾"
Green	3	3½" x 3½" ◸	3¾" x 3¾" ◸
Green	4, 5	1¾" x 3¾"	2" x 4"
Unit B – Make 40			
Green	1	3¼" x 3¼"	3½" x 3½"
Plum	2, 3	4" x 4¾"	4¼" x 5"
Floral	4, 5	1¾" x 3½"	2" x 3¾"
Unit C – Make 40			
Green	1	3¼" x 3¼"	3½" x 3½"
Plum	2, 3	4" x 4¾"	4¼" x 5"
Floral	4, 5	1¾" x 3½"	2" x 3¾"
Floral	6, 7	3½" x 3½" ◸	3¾" x 3¾" ◸
Green	8, 9	3¾" x 3¾" ◸	4" x 4" ◸

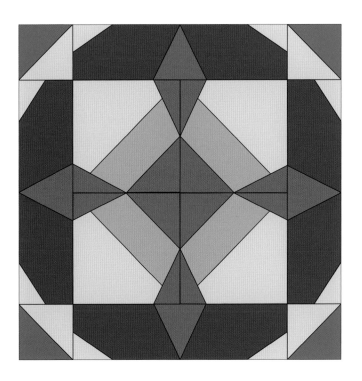

Cotton Fabric Requirements

Floral:	
Blocks	2⅜ yd.
Rose:	
Blocks	⅞ yd.
Cornerstones	¼ yd.
	Total 1⅛ yd.
Green:	
Blocks	2½ yd.
Sashing	1¼ yd.
	Total 3¾ yd.
Plum:	
Blocks	2⅜ yd.
Binding	⅝ yd.
	Total 3 yd.
Backing:	4 yd. – Crosswise
	4½ yd. – Lengthwise
Batting:	2 yd. 90" wide

Cotton Cutting Directions

Note: Strips are cut the width of the fabric; 40" for cotton.

From the floral fabric, cut:

Units B-4 and 5 and C-4 and 5
- 8 – 3½" strips. Cut the strips into 160 – 1¾" x 3½" rectangles.

Units C-6 and 7
- 4 – 3½" strips. Cut the strips into 40 – 3½" squares. Cut the squares into half-square triangles.

Unit A-1
- 6 – 5½" strips. Cut the strips into 40 – 5½" squares. Cut the squares into half-square triangles.

From the rose fabric, cut:

Unit A-2
- 5 – 4½" strips. Cut the strips into 80 – 2¼" x 4½" rectangles.

From the green fabric, cut:

Units B-1 and C-1
- 7 – 3¼" strips. Cut the strips into 80 – 3¼" squares.

Unit A-3
- 4 – 3½" strips. Cut the strips into 40 – 3½" squares. Cut the squares into half-square triangles.

Units A-4 and 5
- 8 – 3¾" strips. Cut the strips into 160 – 1¾" x 3¾" rectangles.

Units C-8 and 9
- 4 – 3¾" strips. Cut the strips into 40 – 3¾" squares. Cut the squares into half-square triangles.

From the plum fabric, cut:

Units B-2 and 3 and C-2 and 3
- 16 – 4¾" strips. Cut the strips into 160 – 4" x 4¾" rectangles.

Sashing, Cornerstones and Binding:

From the green fabric, cut:

Sashing
- 17 – 2½" strips. Cut the strips into 49 – 2½" x 12½" rectangles.

From the rose fabric, cut:

Cornerstones
- 2 – 2½" strips. Cut the strips into 30 – 2½" squares.

From the plum fabric, cut:

Binding
- 7 – 2½" strips.

Flannel Cutting Directions

Note: Strips are cut the width of the fabric; 38" for flannel.

From the floral fabric, cut:

Units B-4 and 5 and C-4 and 5
- 9 – 3¾" strips. Cut the strips into 160 – 2" x 3¾" rectangles.

Units C-6 and 7
- 4 – 3¾" strips. Cut the strips into 40 – 3¾" squares. Cut the squares into half-square triangles.

Unit A-1
- 7 – 5¾" strips. Cut the strips into 40 – 5¾" squares. Cut the squares into half-square triangles.

From the rose fabric, cut:

Unit A-2
- 6 – 4¾" strips. Cut the strips into 80 – 2½" x 4¾" rectangles.

From the green fabric, cut:

Units B-1 and C-1
- 8 – 3½" strips. Cut the strips into 80 – 3½" squares.

Unit A-3
- 4 – 3¾" strips. Cut the strips into 40 – 3¾" squares. Cut the squares into half-square triangles.

Units A-4 and 5
- 9 – 4" strips. Cut the strips into 160 – 2" x 4" rectangles.

Units C-8 and 9
- 5 – 4" strips. Cut the strips into 40 – 4" squares. Cut the squares into half-square triangles.

From the plum fabric, cut:

Units B-2 and 3 and C-2 and 3
- 20 – 5" strips. Cut the strips into 160 – 4¼" x 5" rectangles.

Sashing, Cornerstones, and Binding:

From the green fabric, cut:
Sashing
- 17 – 2¾" strips. Cut the strips into 49 – 2¾" x 12¾" rectangles.

From the rose fabric, cut:
Cornerstones
- 3 – 2¾" strips. Cut the strips into 30 – 2¾" squares.

From the plum fabric, cut:
Binding
- 7 – 2¾" strips.

Flannel Fabric Requirements

Floral:	
Blocks	2¾ yd.
Rose:	
Blocks	1 yd.
Cornerstones	⅜ yd.
Total 1⅜ yd.	
Green:	
Blocks	3 yd.
Sashing	1½ yd.
Total 4½ yd.	
Plum:	
Blocks	3 yd.
Binding	¾ yd.
Total 3¾ yd.	
Backing:	4 yd. – Crosswise
	4½ yd. – Lengthwise
Batting:	2 yd. 90" wide

Sewing Directions

1. Following the position chart sew all fabric onto the units A, B and C.

2. Trim the units leaving a ¼" seam allowance for cotton and ⅜" for flannel.

3. Following the diagram sew units A together.

 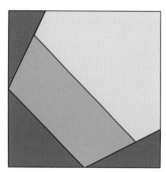

4. After sewing the units A together press all in the same direction. When sewing four units together opposite seams will form, reducing the bulk.

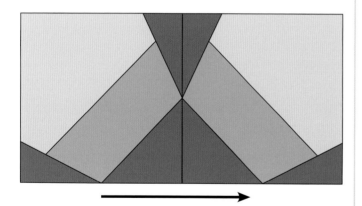

5. Remove only the paper on the back side of the seam allowance; leave the remaining paper on until the block is sewn to the sashing.

6. Sew 4 units A together.

7. Press and remove paper from the back side of seam allowance.

8. Sew units B to units A.

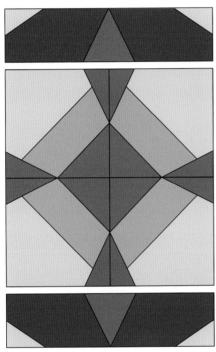

9. Following the pressing arrow, press the units AB.

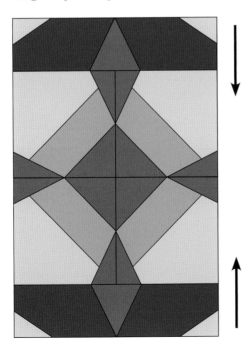

10. Remove the paper from the back side of the seam allowance.

11. Sew units C to units AB making 20 blocks.

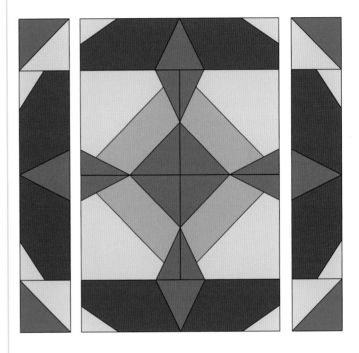

12. Press and remove the paper from the back side of the seam allowance.

Assembling the Quilt

1. Referring to the diagram, sew sashing between the rows of blocks using a ¼" seam allowance for cotton and ⅜" for flannel.

2. Press towards the sashing. Follow pressing arrows.

3. Sew cornerstones and sashing together using a ¼" seam allowance for cotton and ⅜" for flannel.

4. Press towards the sashing. Follow pressing arrows.

5. Sew rows together using a ¼" seam allowance for cotton and ⅜" for flannel.

6. Remove the paper from the quilt

7. Quilt as desired.

8. Trim off excess batting and backing.

9. Sew on binding.

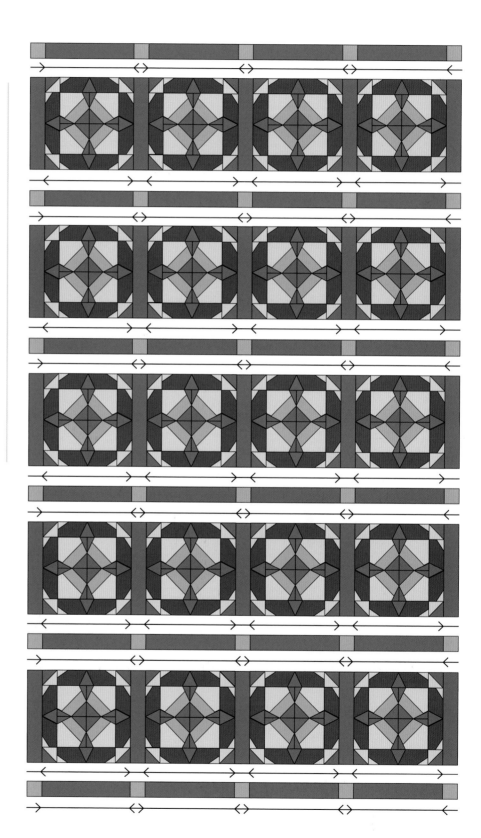

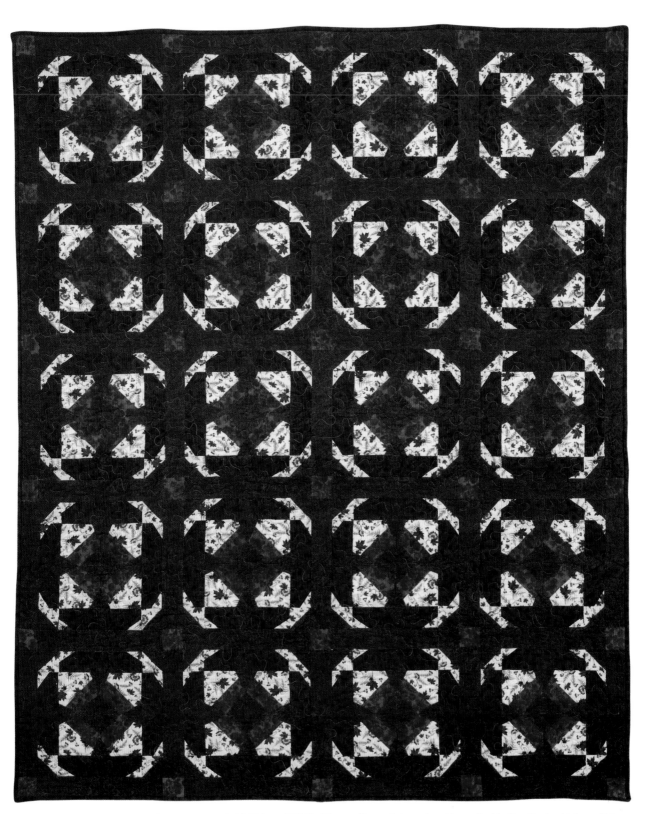

Flannel quilt by Claudia Harrison, Carol Herrick, Julie McClain and Mickie Morgan, Kiowa, Colo. and machine quilted by Pam Statley, Littleton, Colo.

Stars on Parade

Flannel quilt made by Carolyn Cullinan McCormick; quilted by Tracy Peterson Yadon, Manhattan, Mont.

Quilt size: 59½" x 80½" quilted
20 – 12" x 14" Blocks
Number of Copies Needed:
**Unit A – 40
   Unit B – 40
   Unit C – 20
**Note: Use legal size paper (8½" x 14")

Refer to How to Paper Piece on page 9 for any instructions on cutting, assembling, quilting and binding.

Position Chart

FABRIC	POSITION	COTTON	FLANNEL
Unit A – Make 40			
Background	1	5" x 5"	5¼" x 5¼"
Blue	2, 3	2½" x 5½"	2¾" x 5¾"
Background	4, 5	5¾" x 5¾" ◻	6" x 6" ◻
Red	6	1½" x 4¾"	1¾" x 5"
Red	7, 8	1½" x 7¾"	1¾" x 8"
Blue	9, 10	5¾" x 6¾" ◻	6" x 7" ◻
Unit B – Make 40			
Background	1	4½" x 5½"	4¾" x 5¾"
Blue	2, 3	2¾" x 5¾"	3" x 6"
Red	4	1½" x 5½"	1¾" x 5¾"
Unit C – Make 20			
Background	1	3" x 3"	3¼" x 3¼"
Blue	2, 3, 4, 5	2½" x 2½" ◻	2¾" x 2¾" ◻
Red	6, 7	2" x 3"	2¼" x 3¼"
Red	8, 9	1¾" x 5¾"	2" x 6"

Cotton Fabric Requirements

Background:	
Blocks	3 yd.
Blue:	
Blocks	3½ yd.
1st Border	⅝ yd.
	Total 4⅛ yd.
Red:	
Blocks	2⅛ yd.
2nd Border	1⅜ yd.
Binding	⅝ yd.
	Total 4⅛ yd.
Backing:	5 yd. – Lengthwise
Batting:	2 yd. 90" wide

Cotton Cutting Directions

Note: Strips are cut the width of the fabric; 40" for cotton.

From the background fabric, cut:

Unit C-1
- 2 – 3" strips. Cut the strips into 20 – 3" squares.

Unit A-1
- 5 – 5" strips. Cut the strips into 40 – 5" squares.

Unit B-1
- 5 – 5½" strips. Cut the strips into 40 - 4½" x 5½" rectangles.

Units A-4 and 5
- 7 – 5¾" strips. Cut the strips into 40 – 5¾" squares. Cut the squares into half-square triangles.

From the blue fabric, cut:

Units C-2, 3, 4 and 5
- 3 – 2½" strips. Cut the strips into 40 - 2½" squares. Cut the squares into half-square triangles.

Units A-2 and 3
- 5 – 5½" strips. Cut the strips into 80 – 2½" x 5½" rectangles.

Units B-2 and 3
- 6 – 5¾" strips. Cut the strips into 80 – 2¾" x 5¾" rectangles.

Units A-9 and 10
- 7 – 6¾" strips. Cut the strips into 40 – 5¾" x 6¾" rectangles. Cut on the diagonal the long way, from corner to corner. Half of the fabric will be used for A-9 and the opposite half for A-10.

From the red fabric, cut:

Units C-6 and 7
- 4 – 3" strips. Cut the strips into 80 – 2" x 3" rectangles.

Unit A-6
- 2 – 4¾" strips. Cut the strips into 40 – 1½" x 4¾" rectangles.

Unit B-4
- 2 – 5½" strips. Cut the strips into 40 – 1½" x 5½" rectangles.

Units C-8 and 9
- 2 – 5¾" strips. Cut the strips into 40 – 1¾" x 5¾" rectangles.

Units A-7 and 8
- 3 – 7¾" strips. Cut the strips into 80 – 1½" x 7¾" rectangles.

Borders and Binding:

From the blue fabric, cut:

1st Border
- 7 – 2½" strips.

From the red fabric, cut:

2nd Border
- 8 – 5" strips.

Binding
- 8 – 2½" strips.

Flannel Cutting Directions

Note: Strips are cut the width of the fabric; 38" for flannel.

From the background fabric, cut:

Unit C-1
- 2 – 3¼" strips. Cut the strips into 20 – 3¼" squares.

Unit A-1
- 7 – 5¼" strips. Cut the strips into 40 – 5¼" squares.

Unit B-1
- 5 – 5¾" strips. Cut the strips into 40 – 4¾" x 5¾" rectangles.

Units A-4 and 5
- 7 – 6" strips. Cut the strips into 40 – 6" squares. Cut the squares into half-square triangles.

From the blue fabric, cut:

Units C-2, 3, 4 and 5
- 4 – 2¾" strips. Cut the strips into 40 – 2¾" squares. Cut the squares into half-square triangles.

Units A-2 and 3
- 7 – 5¾" strips. Cut the strips into 80 – 2¾" x 5¾" rectangles.

Units B-2 and 3
- 8 – 6" strips. Cut the strips into 80 – 3" x 6" rectangles.

Units A-9 and 10
- 8 – 7" strips. Cut the strips into 40 – 6" x 7" rectangles. Cut on the diagonal the long way from corner to corner. Half of the fabric will be used for A-9 and the opposite half for A-10.

From the red fabric, cut:

Units C-6 and 7
- 5 – 3¼" strips. Cut the strips into 80 – 2¼" x 3¼" rectangles.

Unit A-6
- 2 – 5" strips. Cut the strips into 40 – 1¾" x 5" rectangles.

Unit B-4
- 2 – 5¾" strips. Cut the strips into 40 – 1¾" x 5¾" rectangles.

Units C-8 and 9
- 3 – 6" strips. Cut the strips into 40 – 2" x 6" rectangles.

Units A-7 and 8
- 4 – 8" strips. Cut the strips into 80 – 1¾" x 8" rectangles.

Borders and Binding:

From the blue fabric, cut:

1st Border
- 7 – 2¾" strips.

Flannel Fabric Requirements

Background:	
Blocks	3½ yd.
Blue:	
Blocks	4 ⅝ yd.
1st Border	¾ yd.
	Total 5 ⅜ yd.
Red:	
Blocks	2¾ yd.
2nd Border	1¼ yd.
Binding	¾ yd.
	Total 4¾ yd.
Backing:	5 yd. – Lengthwise
Batting:	2 yd. 90" wide

From the red fabric, cut:

2nd Border
- 8 – 5" wide strips.

Binding
- 8 – 2¾" strips.

Sewing Directions

1. Following the position chart sew all fabric onto the units A, B and C.
2. Trim the units leaving a ¼" seam allowance for cotton and ⅜" for flannel.
3. Sew units B on each side of units C.

4. Press following the pressing arrows.

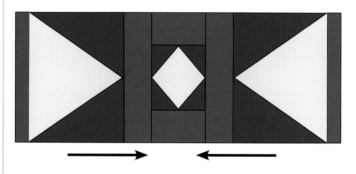

5. Remove only the paper on the back side of the seam allowance. Leave the remaining paper on until the block has been sewn to another block.

6. Sew units A on top and bottom of units BC, making 20 blocks.

7. Press. Remove the paper from the back side of the seam allowance.

Assembling the Quilt

1. Referring to the diagram, sew the rows of blocks together using a ¼" seam allowance for cotton and ⅜" for flannel. Remember to follow the pressing arrows to help reduce bulk.

2. Remove the paper from the center of the quilt but do not remove the paper from the outside edges until the borders have been sewn on.

3. Add the first border to the top and bottom using a ¼" seam allowance for cotton and ⅜" for flannel; press towards the border. Add the sides; press towards the borders

4. Sew on the second border following the same sequence.

5. Remove the remaining paper.

6. Quilt as desired.

7. Trim off excess batting and backing.

8. Sew on binding.

Cotton quilt by Diane Donnelly and Jennifer Lageson, Bozeman, Mont. and machine quilted by Tracy Peterson Yadon, Manhattan, Mont.

Wandering Trails

Flannel quilt made by Carolyn Cullinan McCormick; quilted by Tracy Peterson Yadon, Manhattan, Mont.

Quilt Size: 59½" x 70" quilted
20 – 12" Blocks
Number of Copies Needed:
**Unit A – 80
**Note: Use legal size paper (8½" x 14")

Refer to How to Paper Piece on page 9 for any
instructions on cutting, assembling, quilting and binding.

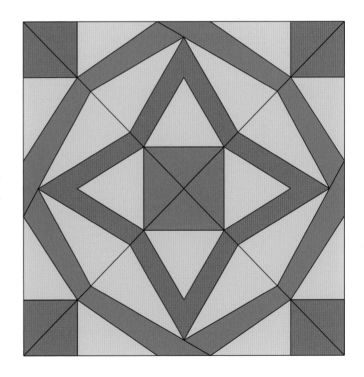

Position Chart

FABRIC	POSITION	COTTON	FLANNEL
Unit A – Make 80			
Background	1	3¾" x 3¾"	4" x 4"
Green Solid	2	4" x 4" ◩	4¼" x 4¼" ◩
Red Print	3	1¾" x 4"	2" x 4¼"
Red Print	4	1¾" x 5¼"	2" x 5½"
Background	5, 6	2¾" x 4¾"	3" x 5"
Green Print	7	1¾" x 5½"	2" x 5¾"
Green Print	8	1¾" x 6½"	2" x 6¾"
Background	9, 10	2¼" x 5"	2½" x 5¼"
Red Solid	11	4" x 4" ◩	4¼" x 4¼" ◩
Red Plaid	12	4" x 4" ◩	4¼" x 4¼" ◩

Cotton Fabric Requirements

Background:		
Blocks		4⅛ yd.
Green Solid:		
Blocks		⅝ yd.
1st Border		⅝ yd.
	Total	1¼ yd.
Red Print:		
Blocks		1¼ yd.
2nd Border		1 yd.
	Total	2¼ yd.
Green Print:		
Blocks		1⅝ yd.
Red Solid:		
Blocks		⅝ yd.
Red Plaid:		
Blocks		⅝ yd.
Green Plaid:		
Binding		¾ yd.
Backing:	4 yd. – Crosswise	
	4½ yd. – Lengthwise	
Batting:	2 yd. 90" wide	

Cotton Cutting Directions

Note: Strips are cut the width of the fabric; 40" for cotton.

From the background fabric, cut:

Unit A-1
- 8 – 3¾" strips. Cut the strips into 80 – 3¾" squares.

Units A-5 and 6
- 12 – 4¾" strips. Cut the strips into 160 – 2¾" x 4¾" rectangles.

Units A-9 and 10
- 10 – 5" strips. Cut the strips into 160 – 2¼" x 5" rectangles.

From the green solid fabric, cut:

Unit A– 2
- 4 – 4" strips. Cut the strips into 40 – 4" squares. Cut squares into half-square triangles.

From the red print fabric, cut:

Unit A-3
- 4 – 4" strips. Cut the strips into 80 – 1¾" x 4" rectangles.

Unit A-4
- 4 – 5¼" strips. Cut the strips into 80 – 1¾" x 5¼" rectangles.

From the green print fabric, cut:

Unit A-7
- 4 – 5½" strips. Cut the strips into 80 – 1¾" x 5½" rectangles.

Unit A-8
- 4 – 6½" strips. Cut the strips into 80 – 1¾" x 6½" rectangles.

From the red solid fabric, cut:

Unit A-11
- 4 – 4" strips. Cut the strips into 40 – 4" squares. Cut squares into half-square triangles.

From the red plaid fabric, cut:

Unit A-12
- 4 – 4" strips. Cut the strips into 40 – 4" squares. Cut squares into half-square triangles.

Borders and Binding:

From the green solid fabric, cut:

1st Border
- 7 – 2½" strips.

From the red print fabric, cut:

2nd Border
- 7 – 4¾" strips.

From the green plaid fabric, cut:

Binding
- 8 – 2½" strips.

Flannel Cutting Directions

Note: Strips are cut the width of the fabric; 38" for flannel.

From the background fabric, cut:

Unit A-1
- 9 – 4" strips. Cut the strips into 80 – 4" squares.

Units A-5 and 6
- 14 – 5" strips. Cut the strips into 160 – 3" x 5" rectangles.

Units A-9 and 10
- 12 – 5¼" strips. Cut the strips into 160 – 2½" x 5¼" rectangles.

From the green solid fabric, cut:

Unit A-2
- 5 – 4¼" strips. Cut the strips into 40 – 4¼" squares. Cut squares into half-square triangles.

From the red print fabric, cut:

Unit A-3
- 5 – 4¼" strips. Cut the strips into 80 – 2" x 4¼" rectangles.

Unit A-4
- 5 – 5½" strips. Cut the strips into 80 – 2" x 5½" rectangles.

From the green print fabric, cut:

Unit A-7
- 5 – 5¾" strips. Cut the strips into 80 – 2" x 5¾" rectangles.

Unit A-8
- 5 – 6¾" strips. Cut the strips into 80 – 2" x 6¾" rectangles.

From the red solid fabric, cut:

Unit A-11
- 5 – 4¼" strips. Cut the strips into 40 - 4¼" squares. Cut squares into half-square triangles.

From the red plaid fabric, cut:

Unit A-12
- 5 – 4¼" strips. Cut the strips into 40 – 4¼" squares. Cut squares into half-square triangles.

Borders and Binding:

From the green solid fabric, cut:

1st Border
- 7 – 2¾" strips.

From the red print fabric, cut:

2nd Border
- 7 – 5" strips.

From the green plaid fabric, cut:

Binding
- 8 – 2¾" strips.

Flannel Fabric Requirements

Background:	
Blocks	5 yd.
Green Solid:	
Blocks	¾ yd.
1st Border	¾ yd.
	Total 1½ yd.
Red Print:	
Blocks	1⅝ yd.
2nd Border	1¼ yd.
	Total 2⅞ yd.
Green Print:	
Blocks	2⅛ yd.
Red Solid:	
Blocks	¾ yd.
Red Plaid:	
Blocks	¾ yd.
Green Plaid:	
Binding	¾ yd.
Backing:	4 yd. – Crosswise
	4½ yd. – Lengthwise
Batting:	2 yd. 90" wide

Sewing Directions

1. Following the position chart sew all fabric onto the units A.

2. Trim the units leaving a ¼" seam allowance for cotton and ⅜" for flannel.

3. Sew units A together.

4. After sewing units A together press all seams in the same direction. When sewing four units together opposite seams will form, reducing the bulk.

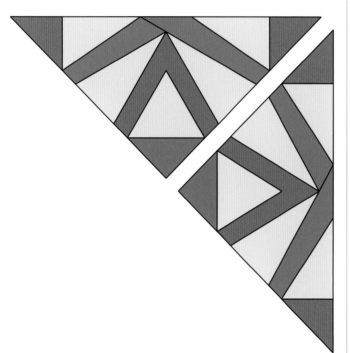

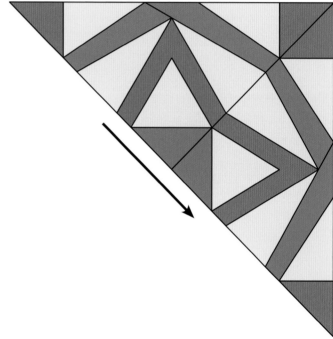

5. Remove only the paper on the back side of the seam allowance. Leave the remaining paper on until you sew the block to another block.

6. Sew all units together making 20 blocks.

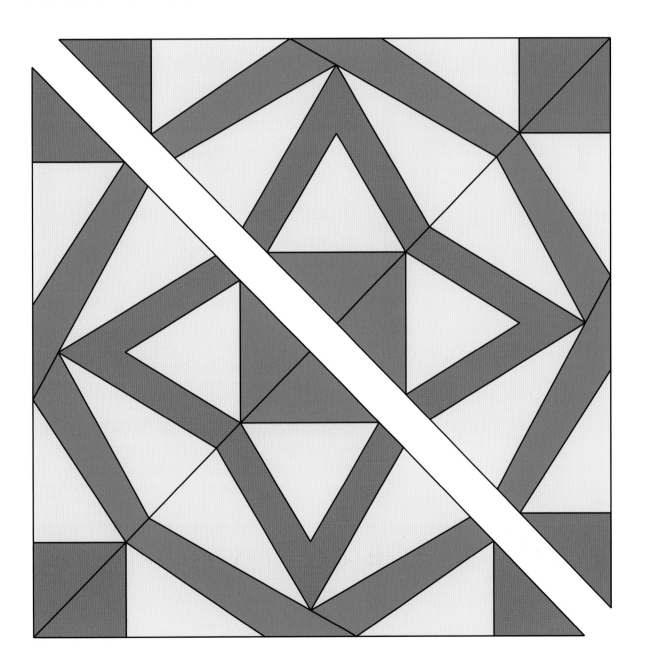

Assembling the Quilt

1. Referring to the diagram, sew the rows of blocks together using a ¼" seam allowance for cotton and ⅜" for flannel. Remember to follow the pressing arrows to help reduce bulk.

2. Remove the paper from the center of the quilt but do not remove the paper from the outside edges until the borders have been sewn on.

3. Add the first border to the top and bottom using a ¼" seam allowance for cotton and ⅜" for flannel; press towards the border. Add the sides; press towards the border.

4. Sew on the second border following the same sequence.

5. Remove the remaining paper.

6. Quilt as desired.

7. Trim off excess batting and backing.

8. Sew on binding.

Cotton quilt by Evie Scott and Nancy Orth, Kiowa, Colo., Polly Rodriquez, Bennett, Colo. and Carol Keams, Elizabeth, Colo. and machine quilted by Evie Scott, Kiowa, Colo. and Polly Rodriquez, Bennett, Colo.

Winter Sky

Cotton quilt made by Carolyn Cullinan McCormick; quilted by Tracy Peterson Yadon, Manhattan, Mont.

Quilt Size: 58½" x 69½" quilted
20 – 12" Blocks
Number of Copies Needed:
Unit A – 80
Unit B – 80
Unit C – 80
Unit D – 80

Refer to How to Paper Piece on page 9 for any
instructions on cutting, assembling, quilting and binding.

Position Chart

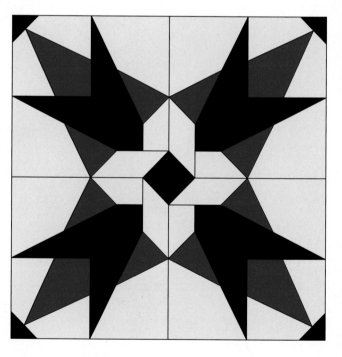

FABRIC	POSITION	COTTON	FLANNEL
Unit A – Make 80			
Red	1	3½" x 3½"	3¾" x 3¾"
Background	2, 3	2¼" x 3¾"	2½" x 4"
Black	4	2¾" x 2¾" ◨	3" x 3" ◨
Black	5	2½" x 4"	2¾" x 4¼"
Black	6	2¾" x 6¼"	3" x 6½"
Units B & C – Make 80 of each			
Background	1	4¼" x 4¼"	4½" x 4½"
Red	2	2¼" x 3¾"	2½" x 4"
Unit D – Make 80			
Black	1	2¾" x 2¾" ◨	3" x 3" ◨
Background	2	2" x 3¼"	2¼" x 3½"
Background	3	1¾" x 4¼"	2" x 4½"
Black	4	2¾" x 2¾" ◨	3" x 3" ◨

Cotton Fabric Requirements

Background:	
Blocks	4¼ yd.
Red:	
Blocks	2 ⅛ yd.
2nd Border	1 yd.
	Total 3 ⅛ yd.
Black:	
Blocks	2 ⅝ yd.
1st Border	⅝ yd.
Binding	⅝ yd.
	Total 3 ⅞ yd.
Backing:	3¾ yd. – Crosswise
	4¼ yd. – Lengthwise
Batting:	2 yd. 90" wide

Cotton Cutting Directions

Note: Strips are cut the width of the fabric; 40" for cotton.

From the background fabric, cut:

Unit D-2
- 4 – 3¼" strips. Cut the strips into 80 – 2" x 3¼" rectangles.

Units A-2 and 3
- 10 – 3¾" strips. Cut the strips into 160 – 2¼" x 3¾" rectangles.

Units B and C-1
- 18 – 4¼" strips. Cut the strips into 160 – 4¼" squares.

Unit D-3
- 4 – 4¼" strips. Cut the strips into 80 – 1¾" x 4¼" rectangles.

From the red fabric, cut:

Unit A-1
- 8 – 3½" strips. Cut the strips into 80 – 3½" squares.

Units B and C-2
- 10 – 3¾" strips. Cut the strips into 160 – 2¼" x 3¾" rectangles.

From the black fabric, cut:

Units A-4 and Units D-1 and 4
- 9 – 2¾" strips. Cut the strips into 120 – 2¾" squares. Cut the squares into half-square triangles.

Unit A-5
- 5 – 4" strips. Cut the strips into 80 – 2½" x 4" rectangles.

Unit A-6
- 6 – 6¼" strips. Cut the strips into 80 – 2¾" x 6¼" rectangles.

Borders and Binding:

From the black fabric, cut:

1st Border
- 6 – 2½" strips.

Binding
- 7 – 2½" strips.

From the red fabric, cut:

2nd Border
- 7 – 4½" strips.

Flannel Cutting Directions

Note: Strips are cut the width of the fabric; 38" for flannel.

From the background fabric, cut:

Unit D-2
- 5 – 3½" strips. Cut the strips into 80 – 2¼" x 3½" rectangles.

Units A-2 and 3
- 11 – 4" strips. Cut the strips into 160 – 2½" x 4" rectangles.

Units B and C-1
- 20 – 4½" strips. Cut the strips into 160 – 4½" squares.

Unit D-3
- 5 – 4½" strips. Cut the strips into 80 – 2" x 4½" rectangles.

From the red fabric, cut:

Unit A-1
- 8 – 3¾" strips. Cut the strips into 80 – 3¾" squares.

Units B and C-2
- 11 – 4" strips. Cut the strips into 160 – 2½" x 4" rectangles.

From the black fabric, cut:

Units A-4 and D-1 and 4
- 10 – 3" strips. Cut the strips into 120 – 3" squares. Cut the squares into half-square triangles.

Unit A-5
- 7 – 4¼" strips. Cut the strips into 80 – 2¾" x 4¼" rectangles.

Unit A-6
- 7 – 6½" strips. Cut the strips into 80 – 3" x 6½" rectangles.

Borders and Binding:

From the black fabric, cut:
1st Border
- 6 – 2¾" strips.

Binding
- 7 – 2¾" strips.

From the red fabric, cut:
2nd Border
- 7 – 4¾" strips.

Flannel Fabric Requirements

Background:	
Blocks	5 ⅛ yd.
Red:	
Blocks	2 ⅜ yd.
2nd Border	1 ⅛ yd.
Total 3½ yd.	
Black:	
Blocks	3¼ yd.
1st Border	⅝ yd.
Binding:	¾ yd.
Total 4 ⅝ yd.	
Backing:	3¾ yd. – Crosswise
	4¼ yd. – Lengthwise
Batting:	2 yd. 90" wide

Sewing Directions

1. Following the position chart sew all fabric onto the units A, B, C and D.

2. Trim the units leaving a ¼" seam allowance for cotton and ⅜" for flannel.

3. Sew units A to units B.

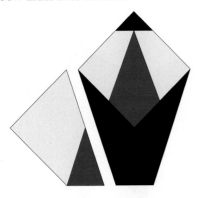

4. Press units B towards units A.

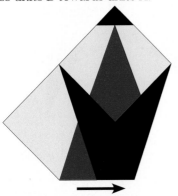

5. Sew units C to units AB.

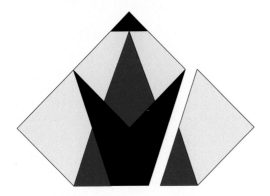

6. Press unit A towards unit C. By pressing this way opposite seams will form when you sew the blocks together.

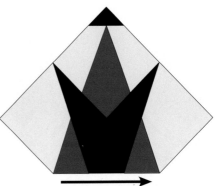

7. Remove only the paper on the back side of the seam allowance. Leave the remaining paper on until the block is sewn to another block.

8. Sew units D to units ABC.

9. Press half of the units A, B, C and D one direction. Press the other half the opposite direction.

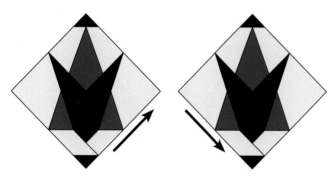

10. Remove only the paper on the back side of the seam allowance.

11. Sew two units of A, B, C and D together.

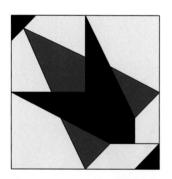

12. After sewing the units A, B, C and D together press all the same direction.

13. Remove only the paper on the back side of the seam allowance.

14. Sew all units together, making 20 blocks.

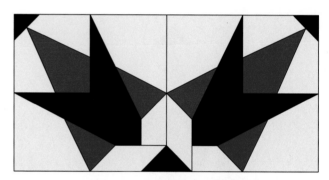

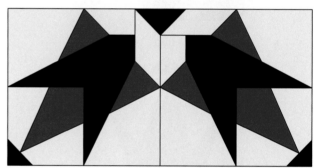

Assembling the Quilt

1. Referring to the diagram, sew the rows of blocks together using a ¼" seam allowance for cotton and ⅜" for flannel. Remember to follow the pressing arrows to help reduce the bulk.

2. Remove the paper from the center of the quilt but do not remove the paper from the outside edges until the borders have been sewn on.

3. Add the first border to the top and bottom using a ¼" seam allowance for cotton and ⅜" for flannel. Press towards the border. Add the sides; press towards the border.

4. Sew on the second border following the same sequence.

5. Remove the remaining paper.

6. Quilt as desired.

7. Trim off excess batting and backing.

8. Sew on binding.

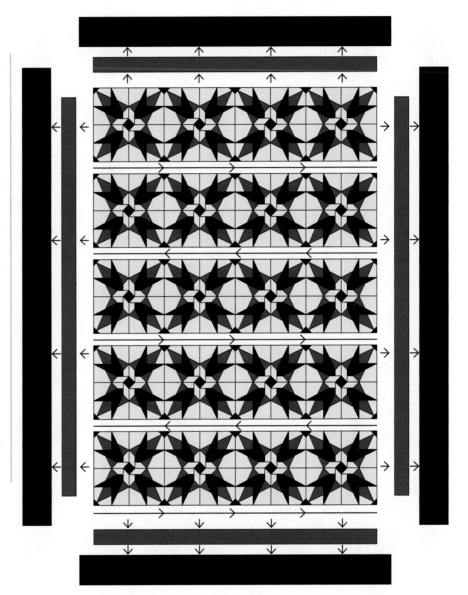

Cotton quilt by Maryellen Joga, Castle Rock, Colo., and machine quilted by Diane Varner, Elizabeth, Colo.

Winter Sky

Cotton quilt made by Carolyn Cullinan McCormick; quilted by Tracy Peterson Yadon, Manhattan, Mont.

Quilt Size: 58½" x 69½" quilted
20 – 12" Blocks
Number of Copies Needed:
Unit A – 80
Unit B – 80
Unit C – 80
Unit D – 80

Refer to How to Paper Piece on page 9 for any
instructions on cutting, assembling, quilting and binding.

Position Chart

FABRIC	POSITION	COTTON	FLANNEL
Unit A – Make 80			
Red	1	3½" x 3½"	3¾" x 3¾"
Background	2, 3	2¼" x 3¾"	2½" x 4"
Black	4	2¾" x 2¾" ◲	3" x 3" ◲
Black	5	2½" x 4"	2¾" x 4¼"
Black	6	2¾" x 6¼"	3" x 6½"
Units B & C – Make 80 of each			
Background	1	4¼" x 4¼"	4½" x 4½"
Red	2	2¼" x 3¾"	2½" x 4"
Unit D – Make 80			
Black	1	2¾" x 2¾" ◲	3" x 3" ◲
Background	2	2" x 3¼"	2¼" x 3½"
Background	3	1¾" x 4¼"	2" x 4½"
Black	4	2¾" x 2¾" ◲	3" x 3" ◲

Cotton Fabric Requirements

Background:	
Blocks	4¼ yd.
Red:	
Blocks	2⅛ yd.
2nd Border	1 yd.
	Total 3⅛ yd.
Black:	
Blocks	2⅝ yd.
1st Border	⅝ yd.
Binding	⅝ yd.
	Total 3⅞ yd.
Backing:	3¾ yd. – Crosswise
	4¼ yd. – Lengthwise
Batting:	2 yd. 90" wide

Cotton Cutting Directions

Note: Strips are cut the width of the fabric; 40" for cotton.

From the background fabric, cut:

Unit D-2
- 4 – 3¼" strips. Cut the strips into 80 – 2" x 3¼" rectangles.

Units A-2 and 3
- 10 – 3¾" strips. Cut the strips into 160 – 2¼" x 3¾" rectangles.

Units B and C-1
- 18 – 4¼" strips. Cut the strips into 160 – 4¼" squares.

Unit D-3
- 4 – 4¼" strips. Cut the strips into 80 – 1¾" x 4¼" rectangles.

From the red fabric, cut:

Unit A-1
- 8 – 3½" strips. Cut the strips into 80 – 3½" squares.

Units B and C-2
- 10 – 3¾" strips. Cut the strips into 160 – 2¼" x 3¾" rectangles.

From the black fabric, cut:

Units A-4 and Units D-1 and 4
- 9 – 2¾" strips. Cut the strips into 120 – 2¾" squares. Cut the squares into half-square triangles.

Unit A-5
- 5 – 4" strips. Cut the strips into 80 – 2½" x 4" rectangles.

Unit A-6
- 6 – 6¼" strips. Cut the strips into 80 – 2¾" x 6¼" rectangles.

Borders and Binding:

From the black fabric, cut:

1st Border
- 6 – 2½" strips.

Binding
- 7 – 2½" strips.

From the red fabric, cut:

2nd Border
- 7 – 4½" strips.

Flannel Cutting Directions

Note: Strips are cut the width of the fabric; 38" for flannel.

From the background fabric, cut:

Unit D-2
- 5 – 3½" strips. Cut the strips into 80 – 2¼" x 3½" rectangles.

Units A-2 and 3
- 11 – 4" strips. Cut the strips into 160 – 2½" x 4" rectangles.

Units B and C-1
- 20 – 4½" strips. Cut the strips into 160 – 4½" squares.

Unit D-3
- 5 – 4½" strips. Cut the strips into 80 – 2" x 4½" rectangles.

From the red fabric, cut:

Unit A-1
- 8 – 3¾" strips. Cut the strips into 80 – 3¾" squares.

Units B and C-2
- 11 – 4" strips. Cut the strips into 160 – 2½" x 4" rectangles.

From the black fabric, cut:

Units A-4 and D-1 and 4
- 10 – 3" strips. Cut the strips into 120 – 3" squares. Cut the squares into half-square triangles.

Unit A-5
- 7 – 4¼" strips. Cut the strips into 80 – 2¾" x 4¼" rectangles.

Unit A-6
- 7 – 6½" strips. Cut the strips into 80 – 3" x 6½" rectangles.

Borders and Binding:

From the black fabric, cut:

1st Border
- 6 – 2¾" strips.

Binding
- 7 – 2¾" strips.

From the red fabric, cut:

2nd Border
- 7 – 4¾" strips.

Flannel Fabric Requirements

Background:	
Blocks	5 ⅛ yd.
Red:	
Blocks	2 ⅜ yd.
2nd Border	1 ⅛ yd.
	Total 3½ yd.
Black:	
Blocks	3¼ yd.
1st Border	⅝ yd.
Binding:	¾ yd.
	Total 4 ⅝ yd.
Backing:	3¾ yd. – Crosswise
	4¼ yd. – Lengthwise
Batting:	2 yd. 90" wide

Sewing Directions

1. Following the position chart sew all fabric onto the units A, B, C and D.
2. Trim the units leaving a ¼" seam allowance for cotton and ⅜" for flannel.
3. Sew units A to units B.

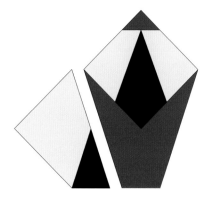

4. Press units B towards units A.

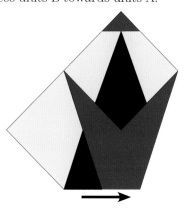

5. Sew units C to units AB.

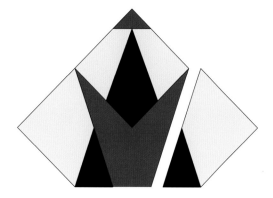

6. Press unit A towards unit C. By pressing this way opposite seams will form when you sew the blocks together.

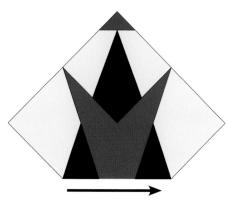

7. Remove only the paper on the back side of the seam allowance. Leave the remaining paper on until the block is sewn to another block.
8. Sew units D to units ABC.

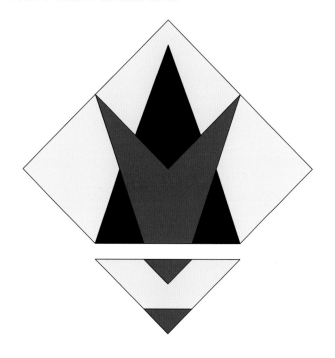

9. Press half of the units A, B, C and D one direction. Press the other half the opposite direction.

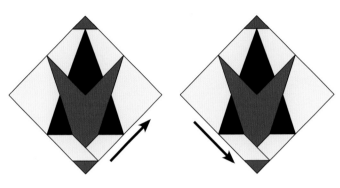

10. Remove only the paper on the back side of the seam allowance.

11. Sew two units of A, B, C and D together.

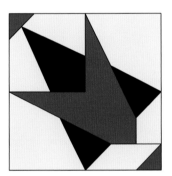 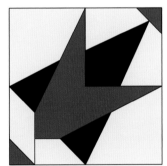

12. After sewing the units A, B, C and D together press all the same direction.

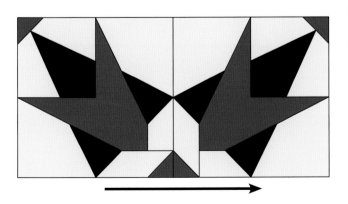

13. Remove only the paper on the back side of the seam allowance.

14. Sew all units together, making 20 blocks.

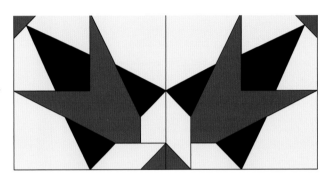

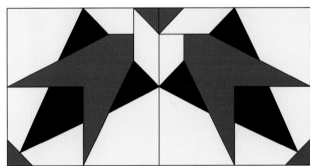

Assembling the Quilt

1. Referring to the diagram, sew the rows of blocks together using a ¼" seam allowance for cotton and ⅜" for flannel. Remember to follow the pressing arrows to help reduce the bulk.

2. Remove the paper from the center of the quilt but do not remove the paper from the outside edges until the borders have been sewn on.

3. Add the first border to the top and bottom using a ¼" seam allowance for cotton and ⅜" for flannel. Press towards the border. Add the sides; press towards the border.

4. Sew on the second border following the same sequence.

5. Remove the remaining paper.

6. Quilt as desired.

7. Trim off excess batting and backing.

8. Sew on binding.

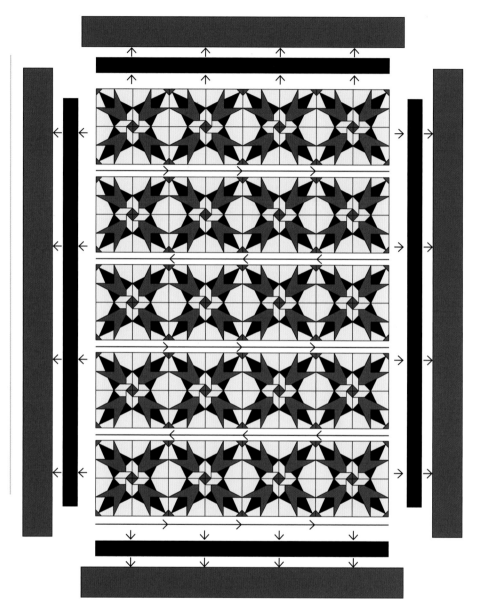

Cotton quilt by Maryellen Joga, Castle Rock, Colo., and machine quilted by Diane Varner, Elizabeth, Colo.

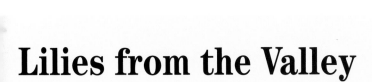

Lilies from the Valley

Flannel quilt made by Carolyn Cullinan McCormick; quilted by Tracy Peterson Yadon, Manhattan, Mont.

Quilt Size: 58" x 74" quilted
12 – 12" Blocks
Number of Copies Needed:
** Unit A – 12
Unit B – 12
Unit C – 12
** Unit D – 12
** Note: Use legal size paper (8½ x 14).

Refer to How to Paper Piece on page 9 for any instructions on cutting, assembling, quilting and binding.

Position Chart

FABRIC	POSITION	COTTON	FLANNEL
Unit A –Make 12			
Background	1	3" x 3"	3¼" x 3¼"
Red	2, 3	3½" x 3½" ◲	3¾" x 3¾" ◲
Background	4, 5	3¾" x 3¾" ◲	4" x 4" ◲
Red	6	2¼" x 8"	2½" x 8¼"
Green	7	4½" x 4½" ◲	4¾" x 4¾" ◲
Background	8, 9	6¾" x 6¾" ◲	7" x 7" ◲

FABRIC	POSITION	COTTON	FLANNEL
Units B & C – Make 12 of each			
Background	1	3¾" x 3¾" ◲	4" x 4" ◲
Red	2, 3	3½" x 3½" ◲	3¾" x 3¾" ◲
Background	4	3" x 3"	3¼" x 3¼"
Background	5	2¾" x 5"	3" x 5¼"
Red	6	2¼" x 8"	2½" x 8¼"
Green	7	4½" x 4½" ◲	4¾" x 4¾" ◲

FABRIC	POSITION	COTTON	FLANNEL
Unit D – Make 12			
Green	1	1½" x 7½"	1¾" x 7¾"
Background	2, 3	2¾" x 6¼"	3" x 6½"
Green	4, 5	1½" x 9¼"	1¾" x 9½"
Background	6, 7	2" x 8"	2¼" x 8¼"
Green	8	2¼" x 4"	2½" x 4¼"
Green	9	2¼" x 5¼"	2½" x 5½"

Cotton Fabric Requirements

Background:

Blocks	2½ yd.
Solid Blocks,	2¼ yd.
Setting & Corner	
Triangles	
	Total 4¾ yd.

Red:

Blocks	1⅜ yd.
Border	1 yd.
	Total 2⅜ yd.

Green:

Blocks	1⅜ yd.
Binding	⅝ yd.
	Total 2 yd.

Backing:	4½ yd. – Lengthwise
Batting:	2 yd. 90" wide

Cotton Cutting Directions

Note: Strips are cut the width of the fabric; 40" for cotton.

From the background fabric, cut:

Units A-1 and B and C-4
- 3 – 3" strips. Cut the strips into 36 – 3" squares.

Units A-4 and 5 and B and C-1
- 3 – 3¾" strips. Cut the strips into 24 – 3¾" squares. Cut the squares into half-square triangles.

Units B and C-5
- 2 – 5" strips. Cut the strips into 24 – 2¾" x 5" rectangles.

Units D-2 and 3
- 2 – 6¼" strips. Cut the strips into 24 – 2¾" x 6¼" rectangles.

Units A-8 and A-9
- 3 – 6¾" strips. Cut the strips into 12 – 6¾" squares. Cut the squares into half-square triangles.

Units D-6 and 7
- 2 – 8" strips. Cut the strips into 24 – 2" x 8" rectangles.

From the red fabric, cut:

Units A-2 and 3 and B and C-2 and 3
- 4 – 3½" strips. Cut the strips into 36 – 3½" squares. Cut the squares into half-square triangles.

Units A-6 and B and C-6
- 3 – 8" strips. Cut the strips into 36 – 2¼" x 8" rectangles.

From the green fabric, cut:

Unit D-8
- 1 – 4" strip. Cut the strip into 12 – 2¼" x 4" rectangles.

Units A-7 and B and C-7
- 3 – 4½" strips. Cut the strips into 18 – 4½" squares. Cut squares into half-square triangles.

Unit D-9
- 1 – 5¼" strip. Cut the strip into 12 – 2¼" x 5¼" rectangles.

Unit D-1
- 1 – 7½" strip. Cut the strip into 12 – 1½" x 7½" rectangles.

Units D-4 and 5
- 1 – 9¼" strips. Cut the strips into 24 – 1½" x 9¼" rectangles.

Solid Blocks, Triangles, Borders and Bindings:

From the background fabric, cut:
Solid blocks
- 2 – 12½" strips. Cut the strips into 6 – 12½" squares.

Setting Triangles
- 2 – 18¼" strips. Cut the strips into 3 – 18¼" squares. Cut the squares on the diagonal twice.

Corner Triangles
- 1 – 9⅜" strip. Cut the strip into 2 – 9⅜" squares. Cut squares into half-square triangles.

From the red fabric, cut:
Border
- 7 – 4½" strips.

From the green fabric, cut:
Binding
- 7 – 2½" strips.

Flannel Cutting Directions

Note: Strips are cut the width of the fabric; 38" for flannel.

From the background fabric, cut:

Units A-1 and B and C-4
- 4 – 3¼" strips. Cut the strips into 36 – 3¼" squares.

Units A-4 and 5 and B and C-1
- 3 – 4" strips. Cut the strips into 24 – 4" squares. Cut the squares into half-square triangles.

Units B and C-5
- 2 – 5¼" strips. Cut the strips into 24 – 3" x 5¼" rectangles.

Units D-2 and 3
- 2 – 6½" strips. Cut the strips into 24 – 3" x 6½" rectangles.

Units A-8 and 9
- 3 – 7" strips. Cut the strips into 12 – 7" squares. Cut the squares into half-square triangles.

Units D-6 and 7
- 2 – 8¼" strips. Cut the strips into 24 – 2¼" x 8¼" rectangles.

From the red fabric, cut:

Units A-2 and 3 and B and C-2 and 3
- 4 – 3¾" strips. Cut the strips into 36 – 3¾" squares. Cut the squares into half-square triangles.

Units A-6 and B and C-6
- 3 – 8¼" strips. Cut the strips into 36 – 2½" x 8¼" rectangles.

From the green fabric, cut:
Unit D-8
- 1 – 4¼" strip. Cut the strip into 12 – 2½" x 4¼" rectangles.

Units A-7 and B and C-7
- 3 – 4¾" strips. Cut the strips into 18 – 4¾" squares. Cut squares into half-square triangles.

Unit D-9
- 1 – 5½" strip. Cut the strip into 12 – 2½" x 5½" rectangles.

Unit D-1
- 1 – 7¾" strip. Cut the strip into 12 – 1¾" x 7¾" rectangles.

Units D-4 and 5
- 2 – 9½" strips. Cut the strips into 24 – 1¾" x 9½" rectangles.

Solid Blocks, Triangles, Borders and Bindings:

From the background fabric, cut:
Solid blocks
- 2 – 12¾" strips. Cut the strips into 6 – 12¾" squares.

Setting Triangles
- 2 – 18⅞" strips. Cut the strips into 3 – 18⅞" squares. Cut the squares on the diagonal twice.

Flannel Fabric Requirements

Background:	
Blocks	2 ⅝ yd.
Solid Blocks, Setting & Corner Triangles	2¼ yd.
	Total 4 ⅞ yd.
Red:	
Blocks	1 ⅜ yd.
Border	1 ⅛ yd.
	Total 2½ yd.
Green:	
Blocks	1⅝ yd.
Binding	¾ yd.
	Total 2 ⅜ yd.
Backing:	4½ yd. - Lengthwise
Batting:	2 yd. 90" wide

Corner Triangles
- 1 – 9¾" strip. Cut the strip into 2 – 9¾" squares. Cut squares into half-square triangles.

From the red fabric, cut:
Border
- 7 – 4¾" strips.

From the green fabric, cut:
Binding
- 8 – 2¾" strips.

Sewing Directions

1. Before sewing the fabric onto the paper, tape the two parts of unit A together.
2. Following the position chart, sew all fabric onto units A, B, C and D.
3. Trim the units leaving a ¼" seam allowance for cotton and ⅜" for flannel.
4. Following the diagram, sew units B to units D. Press.

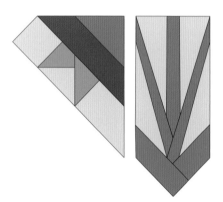

5. Sew units C to units BD. Press.

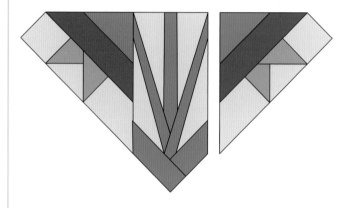

6. Remove only the paper on the back side of the seam allowance. Leave the remaining paper on until you sew the block to another block or setting triangle.

7. Sew units A to B, C and D units. Press.

8. Remove paper from the back side of seam allowance.

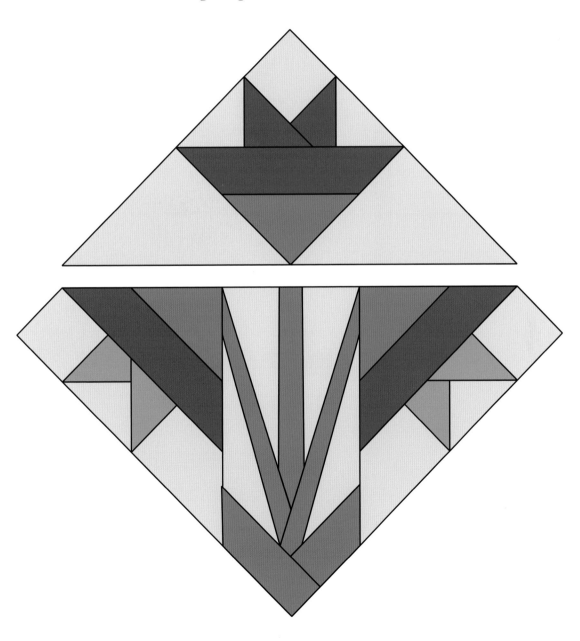

Assembling the Quilt

1. Referring to the diagram, sew the rows of blocks, setting triangles and corner triangles on point using a ¼" seam allowance for cotton and ⅜" for flannel. Remember to follow the pressing arrows. This will help reduce bulk when sewing the rows together.

2. Remove the paper from the center of the quilt but do not remove the paper from the outside edges until the borders have been sewn on.

3. Add the first border to the top and bottom using a ¼" seam allowance for cotton and ⅜" for flannel; press towards the border. Add the sides, press towards the border.

4. Remove the remaining paper.

5. Quilt as desired.

6. Trim off excess batting and backing.

7. Sew on binding.

Cotton quilt made by Kathy Braun, Phyllis Holtz, Corliss Vergeldt, Maureen Simonson, Donna Braun, Dorothy Huehn, Paula Wieser from Rosholt, South Dakota; Deb Ellsworth, Millicent Hannasch, Clarice Grajczyk, JoAnn Sheldon, LaVonne Hellwig, Lorraine Stapleton, Gayle Grimsrud from Sisseton, S.D. and Ruth Bartz from Browns Valley, Minnesota; quilted by Donna Braun from Rosholt, S.D.

Cross Roads

Cotton quilt made by Carolyn Cullinan McCormick; quilted by Tracy Peterson Yadon, Manhattan, Mont.

Quilt Size: 64" x 87" quilted
18 – 12" Blocks
Number of Copies Needed:
Unit A – 36
Unit B – 36
Unit C – 72

Refer to How to Paper Piece on page 9 for any
instructions on cutting, assembling, quilting and binding.

Position Chart

FABRIC	POSITION	COTTON	FLANNEL
Unit A – Make 36			
Blue and Yellow	1	3½" x 3½"	3¾" x 3¾"
Blue	2, 3	3¼" x 3¼" ◨	3½" x 3½" ◨
Blue	4	4½" x 4½"	4¾" x 4¾"
Blue/ Yellow and Yellow	5	**	**
Unit B – Make 36			
Blue and Yellow	1	3½" x 3½"	3¾" x 3¾"
Blue	2, 3	3¼" x 3¼" ◨	3½" x 3½" ◨
Blue	4	4½" x 4½"	4¾" x 4¾"
Unit C – Make 72			
Blue and Yellow	1	3" x 3"	3¼" x 3¼"
Yellow	2, 3	4½" x 4½" ◨	4¾" x 4¾" ◨

** See cutting and sewing directions.

Cotton Fabric Requirements

Yellow:		
Blocks		2 ⅞ yd.
Binding		⅝ yd.
	Total	3½ yd.
Blue and Yellow:		
Blocks		1¾ yd.
Blue:		
Blocks		3 yd.
Border:		⅞ yd.
	Total	3 ⅞ yd.
Backing:	5½ yd. – Lengthwise	
Batting:	3 yd. 90" wide	

Cotton Cutting Directions

Note: Strips are cut the width of the fabric; 40" for cotton.

From the yellow fabric, cut:

Unit A-5
- 3 – 2½" strips.
- **Follow sewing directions on page 94, step 1.

Units C-2 and 3
- 9 – 4½" strips. Cut the strips into 72 – 4½" squares. Cut squares into half-square triangles.

From the blue and yellow fabric, cut:

Unit A-5
- 3 – 2½" strips.
- **Follow sewing directions on page 94, step 1.

Unit C-1
- 6 – 3" strips. Cut the strips into 72 – 3" squares.

Units A-1 and B-1
- 7 – 3½" strips. Cut the strips into 72 – 3½" squares.

From the blue fabric, cut:

Units A-2 and 3 and B-2 and 3
- 7 – 3¼" strips. Cut the strips into 72 – 3¼" squares. Cut the squares into half-square triangles.

Units A-4 and B-4
- 9 – 4½" strips. Cut the strips into 72 – 4½" squares.

Striped Block:

From the yellow fabric, cut:
- 6 – 7½" strips.
- **Follow sewing directions for striped block on page 95, step 11.

From the blue fabric, cut:
- 12 – 3" strips.
- **Follow sewing directions for striped block on page 95, step 11.

Border and Binding:

From the blue fabric, cut:

Border
- 8 – 3" strips.

From the yellow fabric, cut:

Binding
- 8 – 2½" strips

Flannel Cutting Directions

Note: Strips are cut the width of the fabric; 38" for flannel.

From the yellow fabric, cut:

Unit A-5
- 3 – 2¾" strips.

**Follow sewing directions on page 94, step 1.

Units C-2 and 3
- 9 – 4¾" strips. Cut the strips into 72 – 4¾" squares. Cut squares into half-square triangles.

From the blue and yellow fabric, cut:

Unit A-5
- 3 – 2¾" strips.

**Follow sewing directions on page 94, step 1.

Unit C-1
- 7 – 3¼" strips. Cut the strips into 72 – 3¼" squares.

Units A-1 and B-1
- 8 – 3¾" strips. Cut the strips into 72 – 3¾" squares.

From the blue fabric, cut:

Units A-2 and 3 and B-2 and 3
- 8 – 3½" strips. Cut the strips into 72 – 3½" squares. Cut the squares into half-square triangles.

Units A-4 and B-4
- 9 – 4¾" strips. Cut the strips into 72 – 4¾" squares.

Striped Block:

From the yellow fabric, cut:
- 6 – 7¾" strips.

**Follow sewing directions for striped block on page 95, step 11.

From the blue fabric, cut:
- 12 – 3¼" strips.

**Follow sewing directions for striped block on page 95, step 11.

Border and Binding:

From the blue fabric, cut:
Border
- 8 – 3¼" strips.

From the yellow fabric, cut:
Binding
- 8 – 2¾" strips

Flannel Fabric Requirements

Yellow:	
Blocks	3 yd.
Binding	¾ yd.
	Total 3¾ yd.
Blue and Yellow:	
Blocks	2 yd.
Blue:	
Blocks	3 ⅜ yd.
Border	1 yd.
	Total 4 ⅜ yd.
Backing:	5½ yd. – Lengthwise
Batting:	3 yd. 90" wide

Sewing Directions

1. To make strip sets for the center of the block sew as follows:

**Cotton: Sew the blue/yellow 2½" strip to the yellow 2½" strip using a ¼" seam allowance. Make 3 strip sets. Press towards the dark fabric. Cut the strips into 36 – 2½" pieces.

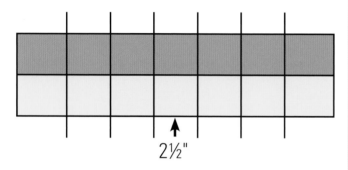

2½"

**Flannel: Sew the blue/yellow 2¾" strip to the yellow 2¾" strip using a ⅜" seam allowance. Make 3 strip sets. Press towards the dark fabric. Cut the strips into 36 – 2¾" pieces.

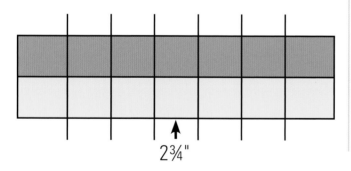

2¾"

2. Following the position chart sew all fabrics onto the units A, B and C. Match the center line of unit A-5 with the seam on the strip set.

3. Trim the units leaving a ¼" seam allowance for cotton and ⅜" for flannel.

4. Sew units A together following the diagram on how to assemble the block.

5. Press all A units.

6. Remove only the paper on the back side of the seam allowance. Leave the remaining paper on until you sew the block to a striped block.

7. Sew units C on each side of units B.

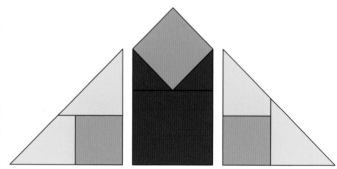

8. Press away from unit B. This will give you opposite seams when you sew unit BC onto unit A. Follow pressing arrows.

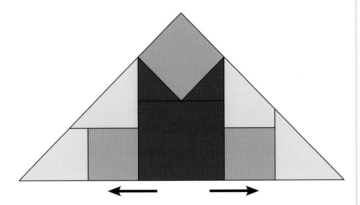

9. Remove paper from the seam allowance.
10. Sew units BC on each side of units A. You will make 18 blocks.

11. To make the strip sets for the striped block sew as follows.

*Cotton: Sew a blue 3" strip on both sides of the yellow 7½" strip using a ¼" seam allowance. Make 6 strip sets. Press towards the dark fabric. Cut the strips into 17 – 12½" pieces.

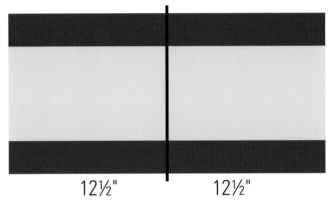

12½"   12½"

*Flannel: Sew a blue 3¼" strip on both sides of the yellow 7¾" strip using a ⅜" seam allowance. Make 6 strip sets. Press towards the dark fabric. Cut the strips into 17 – 12¾" pieces.

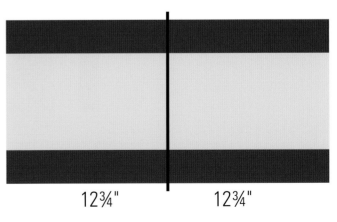

12¾"   12¾"

Assembling the Quilt

1. Referring to the diagram, sew the rows of blocks and striped blocks together using a ¼" seam allowance for cotton and ⅜" for flannel. Remember to also follow the pressing arrows. This will help reduce bulk when sewing the rows together.

2. Remove the paper from the center of the quilt but do not remove the paper from the outside edges until you have sewn on your border.

3. Add the first border to the top and bottom using a ¼" seam allowance for cotton and ⅜" for flannel; press towards the border. Add the sides; press towards the border.

4. Remove the remaining paper.

5. Quilt as desired.

6. Trim off excess batting and backing.

7. Sew on binding.

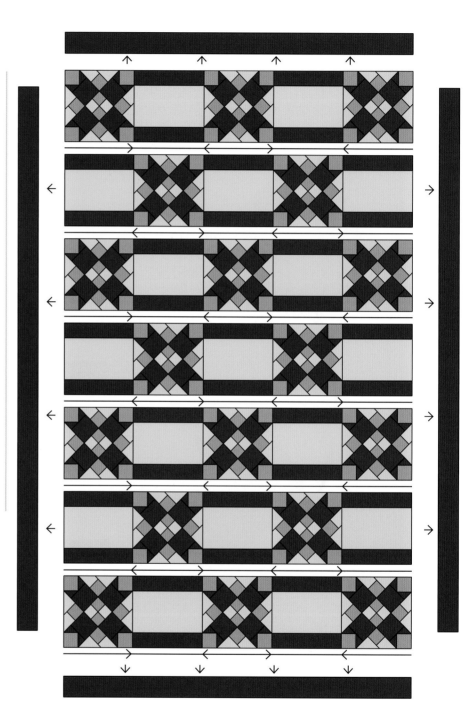

Flannel quilt by Polly Somers and Brenda Phillips, Sedalia, Colo., and Jeannine Glenndenning, Castle Rock, Colo., machine quilted by Wendy Vogel, Highlands Ranch, Colo.

Whispering Pines

Flannel quilt made by Carolyn Cullinan McCormick; quilted by Tracy Peterson Yadon, Manhattan, Mont.

Quilt Size: 57½" x 79" quilted
20 – 12" x 14" Blocks
Number of Copies Needed:
Unit A – 20
Unit B – 20

Refer to How to Paper Piece on page 9 for any
instructions on cutting, assembling, quilting and binding.

Position Chart

FABRIC	POSITION	COTTON	FLANNEL
Units A – Make 20			
Background	1	5½" x 5½" ◇	5¾" x 5¾" ◇
Black	2	2" x 4¼"	2¼" x 4½"
Dark Green	3, 5	2½" x 9¾"	2¾" x 10"
Medium Green	4, 6	2½" x 9¾"	2¾" x 10"
Background	7	7½" x 7½" ◇	7¾" x 7¾" ◇
Rust	8	2" x 12½"	2¼" x 12¾"
Rust	9*, 10*	2" x 13¼"	2¼" x 13½"
Units B – Make 20			
Background	1	5½" x 5½" ◇	5¾" x 5¾" ◇
Black	2	2" x 4¼"	2¼" x 4½"
Medium Green	3, 5	2½" x 9¾"	2¾" x 10"
Dark Green	4, 6	2½" x 9¾"	2¾" x 10"
Background	7	7½" x 7½" ◇	7¾" x 7¾" ◇
Rust	8	2" x 12½"	2¼" x 12¾"
Rust	9*, 10*	2" x 13¼"	2¼" x 13½"

*Sew unit A to unit B before adding pieces 9 and 10.

Cotton Fabric Requirements

Background:		
Blocks		1⅝ yd.
Black:		
Blocks		¼ yd.
Rust:		
Blocks		1¾ yd.
Binding		¾ yd.
	Total 2½ yd.	
Dark Green:		
Blocks		1⅝ yd.
Border		1⅜ yd.
	Total 3 yd.	
Medium Green:		
Blocks		1⅝ yd.
Backing:	5 yd. – Lengthwise	
Batting:	2 yd. 90" wide	

Cotton Cutting Directions

Note: Strips are cut the width of the fabric; 40" for cotton.

From the background fabric, cut:

Units A-1 and B-1

- 3 – 5½" strips. Cut the strips into 20 – 5½" squares. Cut the squares into half-square triangles.

Units A-7 and B-7

- 4 – 7½" strips. Cut the strips into 20 – 7½" squares. Cut the squares into half-square triangles.

From the black fabric, cut:

Units A-2 and B-2

- 2 – 4¼" strips. Cut the strips into 40 – 2" x 4¼" rectangles.

From the rust fabric, cut:

Units A-8 and B-8

- 2 – 12½" strips. Cut the strips into 40 – 2" x 12½" rectangles.

Units A-9 and 10 and B-9 and 10

- 2 – 13¼" strips. Cut the strips into 40 – 2" x 13¼" rectangles.

From the dark green fabric, cut:

Units A-3 and 5 and B-4 and 6

- 5 – 9¾" strips. Cut the strips into 80 – 2½" x 9¾" rectangles.

From the medium green fabric, cut:

Units A-4 and 6 and B-3 and 5

- 5 – 9¾" strips. Cut the strips into 80 – 2½" x 9¾" rectangles.

Border and Binding:

From the dark green fabric, cut:

Border

- 7 – 5¾" strips.

From the rust fabric, cut:

Binding

- 8 – 2½" strips.

Flannel Cutting Directions

Note: Strips are cut the width of the fabric; 38" for flannel.

From the background fabric, cut:

Units A-1 and B-1
- 4 – 5¾" strips. Cut the strips into 20 – 5¾" squares. Cut the squares into half-square triangles.

Units A-7 and B-7
- 5 – 7¾" strips. Cut the strips into 20 – 7¾" squares. Cut the squares into half-square triangles.

From the black fabric, cut:

Units A-2 and B-2
- 3 – 4½" strips. Cut the strips into 40 – 2¼" x 4½" rectangles.

From the rust fabric, cut:

Units A-8 and B-8
- 3 – 12¾" strips. Cut the strips into 40 – 2¼" x 12¾" rectangles.

Units A-9 and 10 and B-9 and 10
- 3 – 13½" strips. Cut the strips into 40 – 2¼" x 13½" rectangles.

From the dark green fabric, cut:

Units A-3 and 5 and B-4 and 6
- 7 – 10" strips. Cut the strips into 80 – 2¾" x 10" rectangles.

From the medium green fabric, cut:

Units A-4 and 6 and B-3 and 5
- 7 – 10" strips. Cut the strips into 80 – 2¾" x 10" rectangles.

Border and Binding:

From the dark green fabric, cut:
Border
- 7 – 6" strips.

From the rust fabric, cut:
Binding
- 8 – 2¾" strips.

Flannel Fabric Requirements

Background:	
Blocks	2 yd.
Black:	
Blocks	½ yd.
Rust:	
Blocks	2½ yd.
Binding	¾ yd.
	Total 3¼ yd.
Dark Green:	
Blocks	2¼ yd.
Border	1 ⅜ yd.
	Total 3 ⅝ yd.
Medium Green:	
Blocks	2¼ yd.
Backing:	5 yd. – Lengthwise
Batting:	2 yd. 90" wide

Sewing Directions

1. Before sewing the fabric onto the paper tape the two parts of unit A and the two parts of unit B together.

2. Following the position chart, sew fabrics 1 through 8 onto both units A and units B.

3. Trim off excess fabric on the top and bottom of the tree as if adding another piece of fabric.

4. Trim the center of the tree leaving a ¼" seam allowance for cotton and ⅜" for flannel.

5. Sew units together following the diagram. Sew the paper together at the top and bottom of the block.

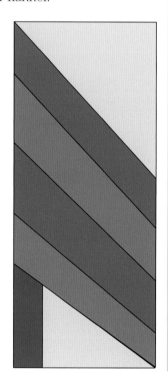

6. Sew fabric on numbers 9 and 10.

7. Trim the outside of the block to a ¼" seam allowance for cotton and ⅜" for flannel.

8. Leave the paper on until the block is sewn to another block.

Assembling the Quilt

1. Referring to the diagram, sew the rows of blocks together using a ¼" seam allowance for cotton and ⅜" for flannel. Remember to follow the pressing arrows. This will help when sewing the rows together.

2. Remove the paper from the center of the quilt but do not remove the paper from the outside edges until the borders have been sewn on.

3. Add the border to the top and bottom using a ¼" seam allowance for cotton and ⅜" for flannel, press towards the border. Add the sides; press towards the border.

4. Remove the remaining paper.

5. Quilt as desired.

6. Trim off excess batting and backing.

7. Sew on the binding.

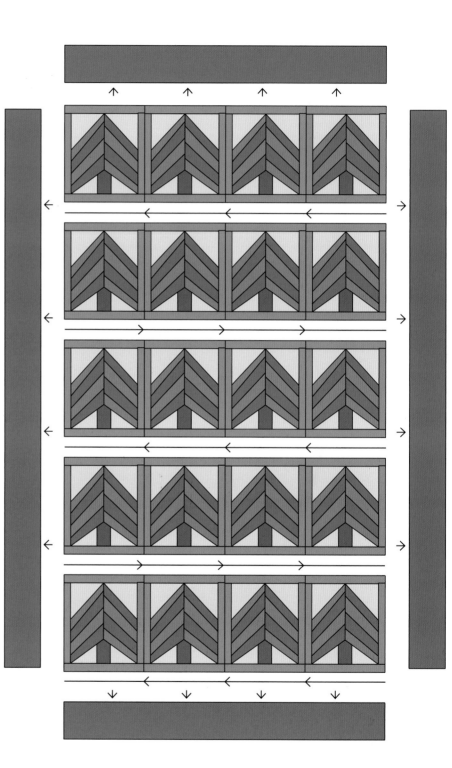

Cotton quilt by Jackie Parker, Castle Rock, Colo., and machine quilted by Carol Willey, Castle Rock, Colo.

Garden Path

Flannel quilt made by Carolyn Cullinan McCormick; quilted by Tracy Peterson Yadon, Manhattan, Mont.

Quilt Size: 66" x 79" quilted
20 – 12" Blocks
Number of Copies Needed:
Unit A – 80
Unit B – 80

Refer to How to Paper Piece on page 9 for any
instructions on cutting, assembling, quilting and binding.

Position Chart

FABRIC	POSITION	COTTON	FLANNEL
Unit A – Make 80			
Floral	1	2½" x 2½"	2¾" x 2¾"
Background	2, 3	2¾" x 2¾"	3" x 3"
Green	4	1½" x 7"	1¾" x 7¼"
Unit B – Make 80			
Floral	1	5¼" x 5¼" ◨	5½" x 5½" ◨
Background	2, 3	2¼" x 4½"	2½" x 4¾"
Floral	4, 5	1¾" x 2¼"	2" x 2½"
Purple	6	2" x 9¾"	2¼" x 10"
Purple	7	4¾" x 4¾" ◨	5" x 5" ◨

Cotton Fabric Requirements

Background:	
Blocks	2½ yd.
Floral:	
Blocks	2 yd.
Sashing	1¼ yd.
	Total 3¼ yd.
Green:	
Blocks	1 yd.
1st Border	1⅜ yd.
	Total 2⅜ yd.
Purple:	
Blocks	2 yd.
Cornerstones	¼ yd.
Binding	¾ yd.
	Total 3 yd.
Backing:	5 yd. – Lengthwise
Batting:	2¼ yd. 90" wide

Cotton Cutting Directions

Note: Strips are cut the width of the fabric; 40" for cotton.

From the background fabric, cut:

Units A-2 and 3

- 12 – 2¾" strips. Cut the strips into 160 – 2¾" squares.

Units B-2 and 3

- 10 – 4½" strips. Cut the strips into 160 – 2¼" x 4½" rectangles.

From the floral fabric, cut:

Units B-4 and 5

- 8 – 2¼" strips. Cut the strips into 160 – 1¾" x 2¼" rectangles.

Unit A-1

- 5 – 2½" strips. Cut the strips into 80 – 2½" squares.

Unit B-1

- 6 – 5¼" strips. Cut the strips into 40 – 5¼" squares. Cut squares into half-squares triangles.

From the green fabric, cut:

Unit A-4

- 4 – 7" strips. Cut the strips into 80 – 1½" x 7" rectangles.

From the purple fabric, cut:

Unit B-7

- 5 – 4¾" strips. Cut the strips into 40 – 4¾" squares. Cut squares into half-square triangles.

Unit B-6

- 4 – 9¾" strips. Cut the strips into 80 – 2" x 9¾" rectangles.

Sashing, Border, Cornerstones and Binding:

From the floral fabric, cut:

Sashing

- 17 – 2¼" strips. Cut the strips into 49 – 2¼" x 12½" rectangles.

From the purple fabric, cut:

Cornerstones

- 2 – 2¼" strips. Cut the strips into 30 – 2¼" squares.

Binding

- 8 – 2½" strips.

From the green fabric, cut:

Border

- 7 – 5¾" strips.

Flannel Cutting Directions

Note: Strips are cut the width of the fabric; 38" for flannel.

From the background fabric, cut:

Units A-2 and 3
- 14 – 3" strips. Cut the strips into 160 – 3" squares.

Units B-2 and 3
- 12 – 4¾" strips. Cut the strips into 160 – 2½" x 4¾" rectangles.

From the floral fabric, cut:

Units B-4 and 5
- 10 – 2½" strips. Cut the strips into 160 – 2" x 2½" rectangles.

Unit A-1
- 7 – 2¾" strips. Cut the strips into 80 – 2¾" squares.

Unit B-1
- 7 – 5½" strips. Cut the strips into 40 – 5½" squares. Cut squares into half-squares triangles.

From the green fabric, cut:

Unit A-4
- 4 – 7¼" strips. Cut the strips into 80 – 1¾" x 7¼" rectangles.

From the purple fabric, cut:

Unit B-7
- 6 – 5" strips. Cut the strips into 40 – 5" squares. Cut squares into half-square triangles.

Unit B-6
- 5 – 10" strips. Cut the strips into 80 – 2¼" x 10" rectangles.

Sashing, Border, Cornerstones and Binding:

From the floral fabric, cut:

Sashing
- 17 – 2½" strips. Cut the strips into 49 – 2½" x 12¾" rectangles.

From the purple fabric, cut:

Cornerstones
- 2 – 2½" strips. Cut the strips into 30 – 2½" squares.

Binding
- 8 – 2¾" strips.

From the green fabric, cut:

Border
- 7 – 6" strips.

Flannel Fabric Requirements

Background:	
Blocks	3 yd.
Floral:	
Blocks	2 ⅝ yd.
Sashing	1 ⅜ yd.
	Total 4 yd.
Green:	
Blocks	1 ⅛ yd.
1st Border	1 ⅜ yd.
	Total 2½ yd.
Purple:	
Blocks	2½ yd.
Cornerstones	¼ yd.
Binding	¾ yd.
	Total 3½ yd.
Backing:	5 yd. – Lengthwise
Batting:	2¼ yd. 90" wide

Sewing Directions

1. Following the position chart, sew all fabric onto the units A and units B.

2. Trim the units leaving a ¼" seam allowance for cotton and ⅜" for flannel.

3. Sew units together following the diagram on how to assemble the block.

4. Press half of the AB units one direction and press the other half the opposite direction. Pressing in the opposite direction will make it easier when sewing the units together.

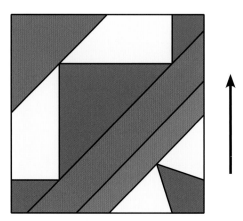

Press 40 this direction.

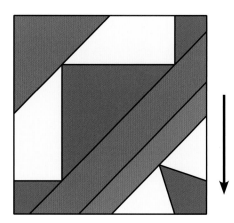

Press 40 this direction.

5. Remove only the paper on the back side of the seam allowance.

6. Sew AB units together.

 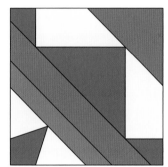

8. Press all the same direction.

7. Remove the paper from the back side of the seam allowance.

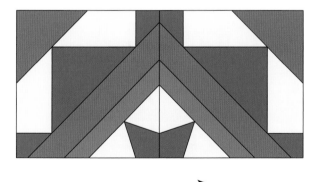

9. Sew all units together making 20 blocks.

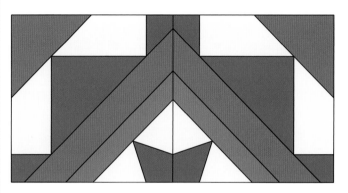

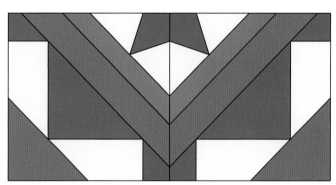

Assembling the Quilt

1. Referring to the diagram, sew sashing between the rows of blocks using a ¼" seam allowance for cotton and ⅜" for flannel.

2. Press towards the sashing. Follow pressing arrows.

3. Sew cornerstones and sashing together using a ¼" seam allowance for cotton and ⅜" for flannel.

4. Press towards the sashing. Follow pressing arrows.

5. Sew rows together using a ¼" seam allowance for cotton and ⅜" for flannel.

6. Remove the paper from the center of the quilt but do not remove the paper from the outside edges until borders have been sewn on.

7. Add the border to the top and bottom using a ¼" seam allowance for cotton and ⅜" for flannel; pressing towards the border. Add the sides; press towards the border.

8. Remove the remaining paper.

9. Quilt as desired.

10. Trim off excess batting and backing.

11. Sew on the binding.

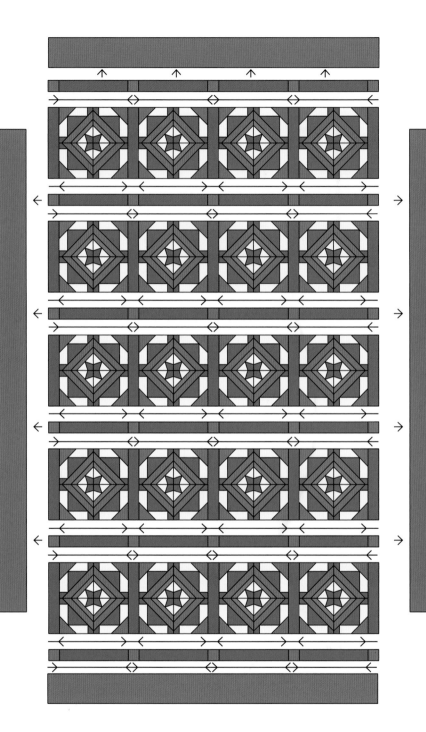

Cotton quilt pieced and machine quilted by Julie Lilly, Monument, Colo.

Whirligig

Flannel quilt made by Carolyn Cullinan McCormick; quilted by Tracy Peterson Yadon, Manhattan, Mont.

Quilt Size: 37½" x 37½" quilted
5 – 12" Blocks
Number of Copies Needed: Unit A – 20

Refer to How to Paper Piece on page 9 for any
instructions on cutting, assembling, quilting and binding.

Position Chart

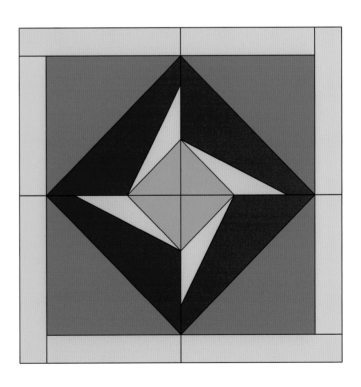

FABRIC	POSITION	COTTON	FLANNEL
Unit A – Make 20			
Turtle	1	6¾" x 6¾" ◻	7" x 7" ◻
Purple	2	2¾" x 8¼"	3" x 8½"
Yellow Plaid	3	1¾" x 5¾"	2" x 6"
Green	4	3¾" x 3¾" ◻	4" x 4" ◻
Yellow Checked	5	1¾" x 6"	2" x 6¼"
Yellow Checked	6	1¾" x 7"	2" x 7¼"

Cotton Fabric Requirements

Turtle:

Blocks	½ yd.
Setting & Corner Triangles	⅞ yd.
	Total 1 ⅜ yd.

Purple:

Blocks	⅝ yd.
Border	⅜ yd.
	Total 1 yd.

Yellow Plaid:

Blocks	¼ yd.
Binding	½ yd.
	Total ¾ yd.

Green:

Blocks	¼ yd.

Yellow Checked:

Blocks	½ yd.
Backing:	1¼ yd.
Batting:	1¼ yd. 45" wide

Cotton Cutting Directions

Note: Strips are cut the width of the fabric; 40" for cotton.

From the turtle fabric, cut:

Unit A-1

- 2 – 6¾" strips. Cut the strips into 10 – 6¾" squares. Cut the squares into half-square triangles.

From the purple fabric, cut:

Unit A-2

- 2 – 8¼" strips. Cut the strips into 20 – 2¾" x 8¼" rectangles.

From the yellow plaid fabric, cut:

Unit A-3

- 1 – 5¾" strips. Cut the strips into 20 – 1¾" x 5¾" rectangles.

From the green fabric, cut:

Unit A-4

- 1 – 3¾" strips. Cut the strips into 10 – 3¾" squares. Cut squares into half-square triangles.

From the yellow checked fabric, cut:

Unit A-5

- 1 – 6" strips. Cut the strips into 20 – 1¾" x 6" rectangles.

Unit A-6

- 1 – 7" strips. Cut the strips into 20 – 1¾" x 7" rectangles.

Triangles, Borders and Binding:

From the turtle fabric, cut:

Setting Triangles

- 1 – 18¼" strip. Cut the strip into 1 – 18¼" square. Cut square on the diagonal twice.

Corner triangles

- 1 – 9 ⅜" strip. Cut the strip into 2 – 9 ⅜" squares. Cut squares into half-square triangles.

From the purple fabric, cut:

Border

- 4 – 2½" strips.

From the yellow plaid fabric, cut:

Binding

- 5 – 2½" strips.

Flannel Cutting Directions

Note: Strips are cut the width of the fabric; 38" for flannel.

From the turtle fabric, cut:
Unit A-1
- 3 – 7" strips. Cut the strips into 10 – 7" squares. Cut the squares into half-square triangles.

From the purple fabric, cut:
Unit A-2
- 2 – 8½" strips. Cut the strips into 20 – 3" x 8½" rectangles.

From the yellow plaid fabric, cut:
Unit A-3
- 2 – 6" strips. Cut the strips into 20 – 2" x 6" rectangles.

From the green fabric, cut:
Unit A-4
- 2 – 4" strips. Cut the strips into 10 – 4" squares. Cut squares into half-square triangles.

From the yellow checked fabric, cut:
Unit A-5
- 2 – 6¼" strips. Cut the strips into 20 – 2" x 6¼" rectangles.

Unit A-6
- 2 – 7¼" strips. Cut the strips into 20 – 2" x 7¼" rectangles.

Triangles, Borders and Binding:

From the turtle fabric, cut:
Setting Triangles
- 1 – 18⅞" strip. Cut the strip into 1 – 18⅞" square. Cut square on the diagonal twice.

Corner triangles
- 1 – 9¾" strip. Cut the strip into 2 – 9¾" squares. Cut squares into half-square triangles.

From the purple fabric, cut:
Border
- 4 – 2¾" strips.

From the yellow plaid fabric, cut:
Binding
- 5 – 2¾" strips.

Flannel Fabric Requirements

Turtle:	
Blocks	¾ yd.
Setting & Corner Triangles	1 yd.
	Total 1¾ yd.
Purple:	
Blocks	⅝ yd.
Border	⅜ yd.
	Total 1 yd.
Yellow Plaid:	
Blocks	½ yd.
Binding	½ yd.
	Total 1 yd.
Green:	
Blocks	⅜ yd.
Yellow Checked:	
Blocks	⅞ yd.
Backing:	1¼ yd.
Batting:	1¼ yd. 45" wide

Sewing Directions

1. Following the position chart sew all fabric onto the units A.
2. Trim the units leaving a ¼" seam allowance for cotton and ⅜" for flannel.
3. Sew units together following the diagram.

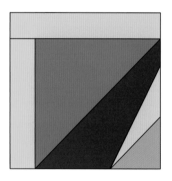 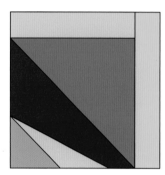

4. After sewing units A together, press all seams in the same direction. When sewing four units together opposite seams will form, reducing the bulk.

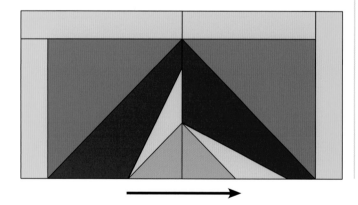

5. Remove only the paper on the back side of the seam allowance. Leave the remaining paper on until the block is sewn to another block or setting triangle.
6. Sew all units together making 5 blocks.

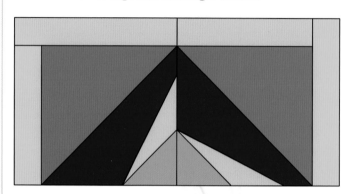

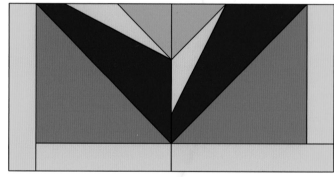

Assembling the Quilt

1. Referring to the diagram, sew the rows of blocks, setting triangles and corner triangles on point using a ¼" seam allowance for cotton and ⅜" for flannel. Remember to follow the pressing arrows. This will help when sewing the rows together.

2. Remove the paper from the center of the quilt but do not remove the paper from the outside edges until the borders have been sewn on.

3. Add the border to the top and bottom using a ¼" seam allowance for cotton and ⅜" for flannel; press towards the border. Add the sides; press towards the border.

4. Remove the remaining paper.

5. Quilt as desired.

6. Trim off excess batting and backing.

7. Sew on binding.

Cotton quilt pieced and machine quilted by Patrice Heath, Parker, Colo.

Sweet Pea

Flannel quilt made by Carolyn Cullinan McCormick; quilted by Tracy Peterson Yadon, Manhattan, Mont.

Quilt size: 58½" x 70" quilted
20 – 12" Blocks
Number of copies needed:
Unit A – 80

Refer to How to Paper Piece on page 9 for any
instructions on cutting, assembling, quilting and binding.

Position Chart

FABRIC	POSITION	COTTON	FLANNEL
Unit A – Make 80			
Green Flower	1	5¼" x 5¼" ◳	5½" x 5½" ◳
Green	2	2¼" x 6½"	2½" x 6¾"
Purple	3	1¾" x 6½"	2" x 6¾"
Green Flower	4	3½" x 6½"	3¾" x 6¾"
Purple	5, 6	1¼" x 4½"	1½" x 4¾"
Green	7	3¼" x 3¼" ◳	3½" x 3½" ◳
Green	8, 9	3¾" x 3¾" ◳	4" x 4" ◳

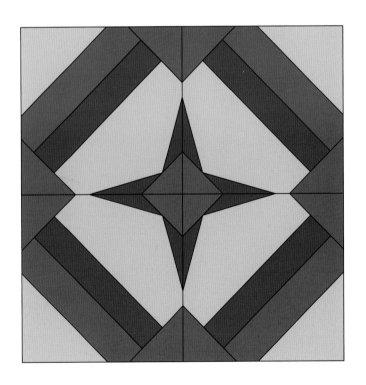

Cotton Fabric Requirements

Green Flower:

Blocks	2 ⅝ yd.
2nd Border	1 ⅛ yd.
	Total 3¾ yd.

Green:

Blocks	2 ⅜ yd.
1st Border	⅝ yd.
Binding	⅔ yd.
	Total 3 ⅔ yd.

Purple:

Blocks	1⅝ yd.

Backing:	4 yd. – Crosswise
	4½ yd. – Lengthwise
Batting:	2 yd. 90" wide

Cotton Cutting Directions

Note: Strips are cut the width of the fabric; 40" for cotton.

From the green flower fabric, cut:

Unit A-1

- 6 – 5¼" strips. Cut the strips into 40 – 5¼" squares. Cut squares into half-square triangles.

Unit A-4

- 8 – 6½" strips. Cut the strips into 80 – 3½" x 6½" rectangles.

From the green fabric, cut:

Unit A-7

- 4 – 3¼" strips. Cut the strips into 40 – 3¼" squares. Cut squares into half-square triangles.

Units A-8 and 9

- 8 – 3¾" strips. Cut the strips into 80 – 3¾" squares. Cut squares into half-square triangles.

Unit A-2

- 5 – 6½" strips. Cut the strips into 80 – 2¼" x 6½" rectangles.

From the purple fabric, cut:

Units A-5 and 6

- 5 – 4½" strips. Cut the strips into 160 – 1¼" x 4½" rectangles.

Unit A-3

- 4 – 6½" strips. Cut the strips into 80 – 1¾" x 6½" rectangles.

Borders and Binding:

From the green fabric, cut:

1st Border

- 7 – 2½" strips.

Binding

- 8 – 2½" strips.

From the green flower fabric, cut:

2nd Border

- 7 – 4½" strips.

Flannel Cutting Directions

Note: Strips are cut the width of the fabric; 38" for flannel.

From the green flower fabric, cut:

Unit A-1

- 7 – 5½" strips. Cut the strips into 40 – 5½" squares. Cut squares into half-square triangles.

Unit A-4

- 8 – 6¾" strips. Cut the strips into 80 – 3¾" x 6¾" rectangles.

From the green fabric, cut:

Unit A-7

- 4 – 3½" strips. Cut the strips into 40 – 3½" squares. Cut squares into half-square triangles.

Units A-8 and 9

- 10 – 4" strips. Cut the strips into 80 – 4" squares. Cut squares into half-square triangles.

Unit A-2

- 5 – 6¾" strips. Cut the strips into 80 – 2½" x 6¾" rectangles.

From the purple fabric, cut:

Units A-5 and 6

- 7 – 4¾" strips. Cut the strips into 160 – 1½" x 4¾" rectangles.

Unit A-3

- 5 – 6¾" strips. Cut the strips into 80 – 2" x 6¾" rectangles.

Borders and Binding:

From the green fabric, cut:

1st Border

- 7 – 2¾" strips.

Binding

- 8 – 2¾" strips.

From the green flower fabric, cut:

2nd Border

- 7 – 4¾" strips.

Flannel Fabric Requirements

Green Flower:		
Blocks		2 ⅛ yd.
2nd Border		1 ⅛ yd.
		Total 4 yd.
Green:		
Blocks		2¾ yd.
1st Border		¾ yd.
Binding		¾ yd.
		Total 4¼ yd.
Purple:		
Blocks		2 ⅛ yd.
Backing:		4 yd. – Crosswise
		4½ yd. – Lengthwise
Batting:		2 yd. 90" wide

Sewing Directions

1. Following the position chart sew all fabric onto the units A.
2. Trim the units leaving ¼" seam allowance for cotton and ⅜" for flannel.
3. Sew units together following the diagram.

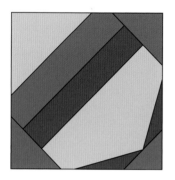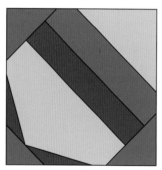

4. After sewing units A together press all seams in the same direction. When sewing four units together opposite seams will form, reducing the bulk.

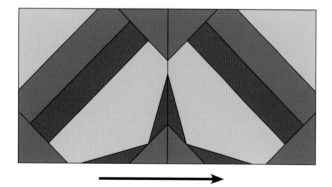

5. Remove only the paper on the back side of the seam allowance. Leave the remaining paper on until the block is sewn to another block.
6. Sew all units together making 20 blocks.

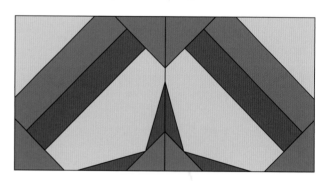

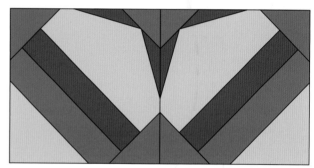

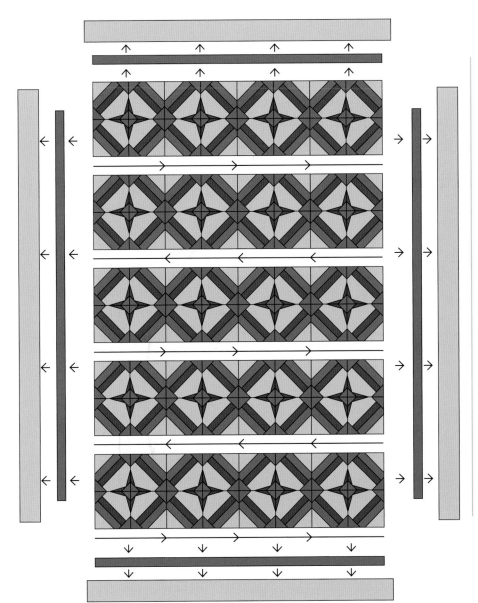

Assembling the Quilt

1. Referring to the diagram, sew the rows of blocks together using a ¼" seam allowance for cotton and ⅜" for flannel. Remember to follow the pressing arrows to help reduce bulk.

2. Remove the paper from the center of the quilt but do not remove the paper from the outside edges until you have sewn on your borders.

3. Add the first border to the top and bottom using a ¼" seam allowance for cotton and ⅜" for flannel; pressing towards the border. Add the sides; press towards the border.

4. Sew on the second border following the same sequence.

5. Remove the remaining paper.

6. Quilt as desired.

7. Trim off excess batting and backing.

8. Sew on the binding.

Cotton quilt by Carol and Tom Netwal, Castle Rock, Colo., and machine quilted by Carol Willey, Castle Rock, Colo.

RESOURCES

**ADD-A-QUARTER
AND ADD-THREE-EIGHTHS:**

CM Designs, Inc.
7968 Kelty Trail
Franktown, CO 80116
Phone: 303-841-5920
Web: www.Addaquarter.com

FABRIC:

Reproductionfabrics.com
25 N. Willson Suite A
Bozeman, MT 59715
Phone: 406-586-1775
Toll-Free: 800-380-4611

Windham Fabrics
812 Jersey Ave.
Jersey City, NJ 07310

THREAD:

Superior Thread
P.O. Box 1672
St. George, UT 84771-1672
Phone: 435-652-1867
Toll-Free: 800-499-1777
Web: www.superiorthreads.com

Aurifil Thread
Bigfork Bay Cotton Company
P.O. Box 2581
Bigfork, MT 59911
Phone: 406-837-2399
Toll-free: 866-245-5718
Web: www.bigforkbaycottonco.com

LONG-ARM QUILTERS:

Lady Quilter
Tracy Peterson Yadon
6288 W. Dry Creek Road
Manhattan, MT 59741
Phone: 406-284-3702

Common Threads
Lynnette Siegle and Jan Holden
164 Road 253
Glendive, MT 59330
Phone: 406-486-5644

Colorado Quilting Company
Diane Varner
36159 Winchester Road
Elizabeth, CO 80107
Phone: 303-646-9569
Email: dvquilter@aol.com

Willey Nice Quilts
Carol Willey
1067 Colt Circle
Castle Rock, CO 80109
Phone: 303-681-0312
Email: WilleyNiceQuilts@aol.com

ADDITIONAL RESOURCES

Annie's Attic
1 Annie Lane
Big Sandy, TX 75755
Phone: 800-582-6643
Web: www.anniesattic.com

Clotilde LLC
P.O. Box 7500
Big Sandy, TX 75755-7500
Phone: 800-772-2891
Web: www.clotilde.com

Connecting Threads
P.O. Box 870760
Vancouver, WA 98687-7760
Phone: 800-574-6454
Web: www.ConnectingThreads.com

Ghee's
2620 Centenary Blvd. No. 2-250
Shreveport, LA 71104
Phone: 318-226-1701
E-mail: bags@ghees.com
Web: www.ghees.com

Herrschners, Inc.
2800 Hoover Road
Stevens Point, WI 54492-0001
Phone: 800-441-0838
Web: www.herrschners.com

Home Sew
P.O. Box 4099
Bethlehem, PA 18018-0099
Phone: 800-344-4739
Web: www.homesew.com

Keepsake Quilting
Route 25
P.O. Box 1618
Center Harbor, NH 03226-1618
Phone: 800-438-5464
Web: www.keepsakequilting.com

Krause Publications
700 E. State St.
Iola WI 54990
Phone: 800-258-0929
Web: www.krausebooks.com

Nancy's Notions
333 Beichl Ave.
P.O. Box 683
Beaver Dam, WI 53916-0683
Phone: 800-833-0690
Web: www.nancysnotions.com

EXPLORE NEW TECHNIQUES TO EXPAND YOUR QUILTING

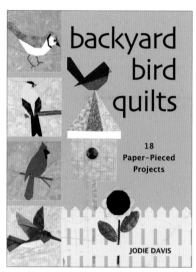

BACKYARD BIRD QUILTS

18 Paper-Pieced Projects

by Jodie Davis

Create 18 beautiful projects including pillows and table runners, each featuring a perfect pairing of rich colors and stunning bird designs. More than 150 color photos and full-size paper-piecing patterns included.

Softcover • 8¼ x 10⅞ • 160 pages
120 b&w template patterns • 150+ color photos
Item# BBQD • $24.99

ELEGANT MACHINE QUILTING

Innovative Heirloom Quilting using Any Sewing Machine

by Joanie Zeier Poole

Heirloom machine quilting can be done on a standard sewing machine. Incorporate the techniques into 20 simple projects such as napkins, table runners, wall hangings and coasters, featured in the full-size quilting patterns.

Softcover • 8¼ x 10⅞ • 144 pages
200 color photos and illus.
Item# ELMQ • $24.99

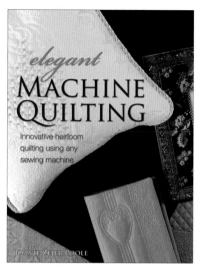

QUILTING FOR THE MEN IN YOUR LIFE

24 Quilted Projects to Fit His Style

by Pearl Louise Krush

Provides simple step-by-step instructions for creating 24 projects with masculine appeal, constructed from flannels and 100% cotton fabrics featuring primary and earth tones. Full-size patterns are included for quilts and related home décor projects.

Softcover • 8¼ x 10⅞ • 128 pages
100 color photos, 150 illus.
Item# MMQ • $22.99

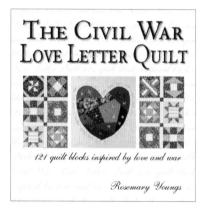

THE CIVIL WAR LOVE LETTER QUILT

121 Quilt Blocks Inspired by Love and War

by Rosemary Youngs

Third in a unique series of historical letter and quilt books, this guide features 121 different paper-pieced block patterns, and related letters. All the block patterns in this book are interchangeable with those in the other books of the series.

Softcover • 8 x 8 • 288 pages
20 color photos, 300 color illus.
Item# Z0751 • $22.99

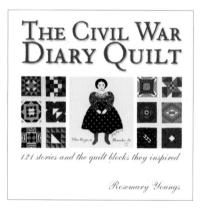

THE CIVIL WAR DIARY QUILT

121 Stories and The Quilt Blocks They Inspired

by Rosemary Youngs

This book helps you bring the past alive with distinctive and exquisite quilt blocks that tell the stories of 10 women living and surviving the Civil War. Explore diary entries of each woman, plus instructions for 121 related quilt blocks.

Softcover • 8 x 8 • 288 pages
121 color illustrations
Item# CWQD • $22.99